D1291600

Mandate
for White Christians

BY KYLE HASELDEN

 JOHN KNOX PRESS
Richmond, Virginia

. . . to Kyle, Alice, Thomas
and to Carol

Scripture quotations are from the *Revised Standard Version of the Bible*, copyrighted 1946 and 1952.

LIBRARY OF CONGRESS CATALOG CARD NUMBER: 66–12595
© M. E. BRATCHER 1966
PRINTED IN THE UNITED STATES OF AMERICA
3575

CONTENTS

791192

LIBRARY
ALMA COLLEGE
ALMA, MICHIGAN

Foreword by Martin Luther King, Jr.

MANDATE FOR WHITE CHRISTIANS is a probingly analytic and compellingly inspiring work. In every sense of the word, it is a great book. I believe that this provocative book constitutes "must reading" for every Christian who yet wonders about what justice demands and love bids him do in personally relating to the civil rights endeavors of Negro Americans.

In this book, Kyle Haselden focuses sharply upon the relationship of the "white" Christian church to the Negro. Impressively and incisively, the study details both the ancient and the contemporary quandary of white Christians caught on the horns of dilemma as to how they should view and relate to black Americans. The author successfully traces through American history the chord of emotional duality that has characterized "religious" whites as they conceived of and acted upon their conceptions of what was and is the rightful place of the Negro in the societal fabric of this nation. Making good use of documentary evidence and moving from the past to the present, the author sketches a clear and convincing portrait of white attitudes and behavior, a portrait depicting the white Christians' continuing ambivalence and vacillation.

Rewardingly for the reader, Haselden looks trenchantly at the agonizing and puzzling duality which has permeated the race relations posture of the American Christian church all the way back to the colonial epoch. The author demonstrates vividly the church's quandary as manifested, for example, in the contrasting positions of its divergent sectors regarding the merits of slavery. The writer shows that on the one hand large sectors of American Christendom accepted and accommodated to slavery, utilizing scriptural and pseudo-anthropological writings to prove the subhuman and soulless character of the blacks; and rationalizing slavery as a

Christianizing and uplifting lever for the dark-skinned primitives. On the other hand, the author indicates, other American Christians postulated the inherent worth and dignity for all men, noted the oppressive, dehumanizing and, therefore, unchristian nature of the master-slave relationship, and became the leading opponents against slavery. The fact that the Christian faith fathered the abolition movement is regarded by the author as one of the few redeeming and gleaming features of professing Christians' dark and drearisome dealings with Negroes in the pre-Civil War days. Haselden avows that the schizophrenic, both damning and redeeming, demeanor characterizes white Christendom right up to the present. White Christians, northern and southern, even today find themselves in a quandary about what attitudes to entertain and what conduct to undertake regarding the Negro's continuing quest for justice and opportunity. The author states persuasively that the imperatives of Christianity demand of the Caucasian faithful much more in the way of involvement in, commitment to, and support of the Negro's struggle.

Justice, the writer asserts, demands that the white Christian reconcile himself to a radical refurbishing of the status quo with its inequalities and deprivations which relegate Negroes to the bottom of the American order. Haselden indicates that distributive justice, as the Aristotelian standard aptly sets forth, requires for every man his due, his fair share. Patently, being manacled by slavery, segregation, and discrimination, the Negro has not gotten his fair share of the American pie. The Negro's deprivation has been due in large part to the white Christian church's abdication of its responsibilities and abandonment of its divine mission.

So now, in order to redeem the church from condemnation, the white Christian should and must join in the Negro's quest for distributive justice in jobs, housing, employment, voting rights, law enforcement, desegregated and quality education, etc. Such commitment will often require sacrifice and suffering. Yet, justice demands as much and, more importantly, Christianity's basic and loftiest ethical imperatives challenge us to such commitment. Thus, the white American churchman, being so responsible for the Negro's plight owing to past and persisting sins of omission and commission, is called upon to leave, on occasion, his traditional and often dormant houses of worship and join the revitalized church which appears in the form of marches, pickets, demonstrations, and sit-ins.

Fortunately, just as the author indicates, the prevalent non-violent character of the Negro's struggle affords an ideal standard and weapon around which the white Christian can rally. I heartily endorse the author's concluding note that Christian love "eliminates the gross inequalities men heap upon each other and . . . binds up and heals the deep wounds which separate men from men." This is the message of reconciliation and such is the mandate to white Christians.

Introduction

In an earlier work, *The Racial Problem in Christian Perspective*, I quoted Martin Luther's familiar words: "The countenance of the church is the countenance of a sinner," and applied these words to the sometimes malicious contributions of the white Christian church to the racial problem. In Luther's day and for sometime thereafter the English word *countenance* had a meaning that is now obsolete. The word did not mean then as now merely the face, the look, the visage. In fact the current and popular use of the word carries a meaning—the outward appearance—which makes Luther's judgment a false rather than a true condemnation of the church. For, on the face of it, the church is not a sinner. It prospers in the United States as it has never prospered before. Rich in this world's goods, sumptuously housed, supported by the wise, the powerful, and the noble, the church has in its outward appearance the visible signs of righteous health.

But if we may assume that Luther was precise in his selection of words and that his translator was faithful to that precision, he referred in this saying not to the church's visage but to its bearing, its conduct, and here found proof of the church's sinfulness. What do we discover if we go behind the church's countenance to its people's conduct, escorted there by their relation to the racial problem and to the Negro's struggle for justice? There was need to see the racial problem in Christian perspective. Is there not also a need to see white Christians in the light of the current racial crisis?

Though this book is a mandate for white Christians I also hope that it will help Negroes understand the white man's dereliction. Let me say as plainly as I can to those Negroes who read this work that though I am myself a white Christian I have no interest in generating sympathy for the white man nor do I in the least desire

to soften the judgments due him from God and society. The white
Christian is and has been an oppressor and exploiter of his darker-
skinned fellowman. He is guilty and no white man should attempt
to hide that guilt or to apologize for it. However, I am concerned
that the racial sins of the white Christian be soberly analyzed and
that the white man's racial evils and spiritual dilemmas be understood for precisely what they are. Specifically we need to understand why the gospel of most white Christians halts on the nearside
of the racial line. Why the great gulf between Christian profession
and Christian practice in race relations? Why, despite the flurry of
racial activity among the church's leaders, are so few white Christians at the parish level moving with Christian deeds across the
racial boundary? My purpose in seeking such an understanding of
the white man is not to soften the blows which should fall upon his
oppressive social structures but to make those blows effective.
Obviously the white man is no angel but the Negro deceives himself and compounds his problems if he concludes that the white
man is wholly a devil. The Negro needs to understand the com-
plexity of the white man, so that he may successfully turn the best
in the white man against the worst.

More directly these words are addressed to white Christians and
have two foci: white Christians who as Christians feel no obligation to help liberate and lift Negroes deprived of their rights as
American citizens and white Christians who are engaged in the
struggle for racial justice but who seek ends which are less than
those demanded by the Christian hope for man. That is, these
words are addressed to those Christians who default their Christian faith by their withdrawal from the racial struggle and to those
Christians who, engaged in the battle for racial justice, adopt
methods which default their Christian faith. It is my hope that
these words will help enlist white Christians in the solution of this
nation's paramount social problem and that when enlisted in this
struggle they will serve the cause of racial justice not as social
malcontents or as political revolutionists but as Christians whose
end is beyond justice and whose methods are disciplined by Christian faith.

The Christian life finds its reality not in monastic, pietistic withdrawal but in deep involvement in the world of men and human

affairs. The uses we make of our solitariness may be one Christian dimension, but without social engagement the Christian life becomes too flat, too thin to be credited with reality. The solitary Robinson Crusoe cannot be fully man or fully Christian until Friday's footprints intrude on the beach over which Crusoe presides in lonely sovereignty and until there are two men in relationship instead of one man in supreme aloneness. The Christian is a social being. His life as a Christian may require periodic retreats from the conflicts and struggles of society but the habitat of the Christian life is the world and the world is man and all of his affairs. In aloneness the Christian life sickens and dies.

Even so, involvement is perilous and the more turbulent the social scene becomes the greater is the danger that the conscientiously involved Christian life will cease being Christian, that it will degenerate into subchristian and antichristian forms of social action. In the vortex of change and conflict, society's needs sometimes appear to exhaust Christian resources and seem to demand of the Christian activities which in motivation and method have no Christian sanction, no Christian validity. If Christians do not seek Christian goals and use Christian instruments in the racial struggle, they default their faith and compound the problem. What is the Christian goal? What are Christian instruments?

This book had its beginning in two lecture series which I delivered in the spring of 1965. I am indebted to the American Baptist Theological Seminary, Nashville, Tennessee, and to its president, Dr. Charles E. Boddie, for the privilege of delivering the Garnett-Nabrit lectures, and to the Eden Theological Seminary, Webster Groves, Missouri, and to its president, Dr. Robert T. Fauth, for the invitation to deliver this seminary's annual Alumni lectures. In the summer of 1965 the major part of this work was presented in lecture form at Union Theological Seminary, Richmond, Virginia, at the invitation of Professor Ben L. Rose. Brief portions of this book have appeared in *The Christian Century* and in *The Pulpit* and are used here by permission of the Christian Century Foundation. Other minor parts appeared originally in the *New York Times Magazine* and in *Dialogue*. I am grateful to these magazines for permission to use this material in revised form. I express special appreciation to my secretary, Miss Elaine Kreis, for her competent preparation of this manuscript.

Kyle Haselden
Evanston, Illinois

1

Why Doesn't the Church Do Something?

As racial violence and the white backlash increase in the United States, one question arises sharply: Why doesn't the church do something about the racial problem? This question—simple and appropriate though it is—does not yield to simple answers. In fact the glib, easy answer will invariably be fractional and will sometimes be totally erroneous. Let us at the beginning dispose of some inadequate answers. First, to say that white Christians withhold themselves from the Negro's struggle for justice solely because they are bigoted, cowardly, and hypocritical may indeed describe many indolent white Christians but it does not describe all of them; nor does this easy answer explore and explain the roots of bigotry, cowardice, and hypocrisy in those Christians who are justly described in these terms. Moreover numerous white Christians—fully aware of the plight of Negroes and of their contribution to that plight, keenly sensitive to the Negro's woes and eager to relieve those woes, sincerely committed to a morality of Christian love and justice—nevertheless experience what is for them an inexplicable paralysis when they attempt to act on the basis of their convictions. If challenged they will properly deny that they are immobilized by fear; if rebuked they will confess their racial sins and acknowledge the justice of the rebuke; if chided for the gap between what they profess and what they do, they will admit the gap and seek guidance in closing it. The failure of such Christians to grapple creatively with the racial problem defies easy explanation. Usually they do not themselves know nor do their critics know all the internal deficiencies and the external restraints which incapacitate their Christian intentions and desires.

Take the state which has the worst record in the abuse of Negroes and which in the United States presents the ugliest picture
of white indifference to and detachment from the Negro's quest for
justice—Mississippi. The white people of that state consider themselves the most Christian people in the nation. By the superficial
tests of church membership and attendance, personal piety and
biblical literalism—in their appearance—they have some claim to
this title. Yet Mississippi was in 1964 the last state in the union to
desegregate its public schools in token compliance with the United
States Supreme Court's 1954 desegregation ruling. Mississippi
sired the White Citizens' Councils in its Sunflower County—home
of the racist Senator James O. Eastland and 68 percent Negro—a
movement which the *Montgomery Advertiser,* before it came
under the Councils' pressure, called "the manicured Kluxism." In
Mississippi more than a score of Negro churches have been
burned, evidently by vengeful white people. Mississippi's white
power structure deliberately and systematically keeps qualified Negroes from registering and voting. And in Mississippi white men
murder, intimidate, and oppress Negroes and, even when caught,
pay no debt to society for their crime. The racial evils of this state,
where so far as Negroes are concerned terror reigns, surpass those
of any place in the world, excepting South Africa. Must we conclude then that all Christians in Mississippi are bigoted, cowardly,
and hypocritical? No, as the English statesman Edmund Burke put
it, justice will not let us "indict a whole people." In Mississippi,
too, there are conscientious, courageous, racially alert, and sensitive Christians whose goodwill toward Negroes is caught and
strangled by a net fashioned from many traditional, psychic, and
social strands. They and their churches are not only immobilized
but also muted by historical forces, social pressures, and uncon-
scious personal inhibitions. These conditions neither relieve such
Christians of their Christian duty to Negroes nor exempt them
from judgment. But the condemnation which they deserve should
be accompanied by an understanding which they do not generally
receive. For conscientious Christians who feel that the penalty for
action is more than they can pay, or to whom what is known to be
morally right appears to be practically impossible, inactivity is not
a consoling refuge. On the contrary, it is intensely painful. In his

latest work, *The Heart of Man,* Erich Fromm, dealing with a different matter, described this pain: "If, for reasons of weakness, anxiety, incompetence, etc., man is not able to *act,* if he is impotent, he suffers; this suffering due to impotence is rooted in the very fact that the human equilibrium has been disturbed, that man cannot accept the state of complete powerlessness without attempting to restore his capacity to act."[1]

Granted that there are bigoted, cowardly, hypocritical white Christians, that some people who bear the name of Christian are exploitative, vengeful, and brutal in their dealings with Negroes, that many white Christians nowhere profane their Lord so sinfully as they do in their relation to Negroes, how do we explain those Christians whose earnestness and sincerity exempt them from these charges but who nevertheless are silent and inactive while the Negro suffers? They do not deserve defense, but it will be good for the Negro and beneficial for the church if we can begin to unravel the riddle which in areas of racial conflict combines Christian devotion with unchristian silence and inactivity.

A second quick and therefore questionable explanation of the church's silence and inactivity before the challenges of the Negro's quest for justice holds that Christianity—not merely its application but Christianity itself—defaults the Negro's crusade because as an ideology, a motivating power, and a shaper of social patterns it cannot cope with the massive complexities of racial prejudice and social oppression. We are tempted to attribute this repudiation of Christianity solely to nonchristians—to communists, to atheists, to young intellectuals who have contemptuously repudiated Christianity because of its alleged social failures, to Moslems who claim that Islam rather than Christianity is equal to the demands of racial brotherhood and that Christianity even in its purest form encourages rather than prevents the deep ethnic and racial cleavages which fragment human oneness. Each of these critics—whatever its own gross failures and deficiencies—speaks in its condemnation of Christianity a word which should be humbly examined rather than arrogantly dismissed. Christians who will not listen to the testimony of Christianity's avowed enemies and rejecters will miss a vital truth about their religion, which is that

---

1. Erich Fromm, *The Heart of Man* (New York: Harper and Row, 1964), p. 31.

perversions of that religion are a much more serious threat to Christianity than that posed by its enemies and rivals.

Belief that Christianity—the gospel and the Christian community—is irrelevant to and inadequate for the racial problem— indeed, for any major social problem—has a larger following within the church than may at first seem possible. These Christians would not frankly discredit Christianity as a resolver of racial crisis but what they do say has the same effect. Optimistic about God's ultimate triumph over man's disorder at the end of history these Christians are pessimistic about God's sovereignty in human history. More than that: They also resign all current social events to capricious, demonic forces which are not to be overthrown until the world and human history end. Their personal piety may be impeccable, their devotion to the church exemplary, their evangelizing zeal commendable; but their detachment of their faith from the world of social conflict, a detachment derived from and supported by an otherworldly theology, is as incomplete as it would be if they had no religion at all. The Christian faith, as such Christians see it, enables men to live in the world as the world is. They have no confidence in the power of the faith to create a better world. *Christianity Today,* a fortnightly, fundamentalist magazine, champions this view of Christianity and states it explicitly in a September 25, 1964, editorial. The editorial cited the use of alcohol and tobacco, pornographic literature, and debasing views of sex as "critical social issues" but stated that "the church of Christ has no jurisdiction in the realm of politico-economic legislation. It has no mandate for commitments that fall outside the church's spiritual and moral responsibility, no authority to become involved in controversial social issues." While this magazine, representative of a wide group of Christians, correctly imputes a moral significance to certain personal habits, it is biblically, doctrinally, and historically incorrect is limiting the scope of Christianity and the church to men's personal habits. This fundamentalist journal crams the whole of Christianity into a rigidly limited area of personal piety and ecclesiasticism, stating, "When the church commits itself, or is committed to, debatable politico-economic positions, its authority and competence in ecclesiastical matters will soon be questioned also. Not only do secular pronouncements introduce a decisive influence among Christians, but in the minds of people generally they tend to break down respect for the church and promote doubt about its qualification to speak authoritatively on spiritual and moral subjects." Under this proscription the church could commit itself on no matters which are debatable, extra-ecclesiastical, secular, divisive, or threatening to the dignity of the church. Paul, Savonarola, Luther, Calvin, John Knox, Roger Williams, John Wesley, head a long list of Christians who have courageously spurned such contemptuous restrictions of the gospel and the church.

This kind of Christianity—a Christianity which concentrates on personal piety and which makes aloofness from the world's agonies a prerequisite of piety—does more mischief in human relations than a score of atheistic cults. The Christian who can cloak his racism or his indifference to the racial struggle in a subchristian theology has an advantage over the nonreligious racist. He can appeal to divine sanction to justify attitudes and conduct much less just and charitable than those held and practiced by people who make no pretense of being Christian. He can summon God as his witness that some men were created to be "hewers of wood and drawers of water." He can cite the Bible for proof that God cursed the Negro's ancestors and in them all of their descendants. He can prove in Scripture that God in a moment created the various races just as they now are and ordained their eternal separateness. He can justify his withdrawal from the human arena with the claim that God calls his children out of the world. What a delicious combination this is: a God-sanctioned bigotry against the Negro, a God-ordained reprieve from the dangerous, arduous struggle for racial justice. No one has ever indicted the evils of this kind of Christianity more forthrightly than did Henlee H. Barnette, professor of Christian ethics at Southern Baptist Theological Seminary, Louisville, Kentucky. Speaking to a Southern Baptist conference on Christianity and race relations at Glorieta, New Mexico, Barnette said, "Some clergymen can corrupt the gospel and use it as a weapon to promote race hatred and prejudice. Indeed, I have never known a racist who was an atheist."

Embarrassing as it is we must acknowledge and face the fact that millions of devout, church-going Christians deny that Christianity has any relevancy to the struggle for racial justice or any power, however faithfully it be applied, to achieve racial justice. Scratch such Christians and in some cases not far beneath their theological skin you will find a bigot, a coward, a hypocrite. But in other cases and not infrequently you will find behind the theological façade Christians who sincerely believe that the function of Christianity is limited to man's interior life and to his posthistorical destiny. These Christians, despite their innocence and their sincerity, must be grouped with those who turn Christianity from a blessing into a curse. In her *Autobiography* Margot Asquith relates a conversation between Frank Harris, the Irish-American author, and Arthur James Balfour, the English philosopher and statesman. Frank Harris said, "The fact is, Mr. Balfour, all the faults of the age come from Christianity and journalism." Balfour replied, "Christianity, of course, but why journalism?" There are varieties of Christianity—whether we think of it as a religion or a body of believers—which justify these acid condemnations, and not least among them is that Christianity which piously abdicates all responsibility for what goes on in the world, which in principle agrees with what Christianity's worst enemies say about its irrelevancy and inadequacy, and which in effect contributes to the faults of the age by turning its back on them.

A Christianity which holds itself apart from the racial struggle and offers the people apparently respectable and approved exits from the dangers and contaminations of that struggle deprives the Negro of an ally, adds to his host of enemies, and betrays the heart of the gospel. Apart from the world into which Christ came there is no Christianity. Man does not live in a two-story house with the secular below and the sacred above. As the German theologian Karl Heim put it, there remains "only the ground floor, secular humanity, with its earthly arrangements for the sustaining and regulating of human life."[2] It was into this world that God came in Christ Jesus—from the eternal to the temporal, from heaven to earth, from the pure Word into impure flesh. The idealistic, sentimental Christian, despising the world God loves, tries to reverse this process, to etherealize the gospel and leave the world to itself.

2. Karl Heim, *The Nature of Protestantism* (Philadelphia: Fortress Press, 1963), p. 133.

What to him does this beautiful religion have to do with fetid slums; fatigued, diseased, and smelly bodies; racial humiliations and atrocities; murders, lynchings, and riots? His religion soars above the sordid world in seraphic aloofness. Whatever it is, this is not the religion of one who was born in a stable and died on a cross, shed tears, touched sores, forgave a harlot, wept, and bled. It is indeed the very antithesis and contradiction of that religion which came into the world in Jesus Christ.

But the question remains: Does Christianity itself in its pure strength and pristine form encounter in the racial problem an opponent for which it is no match? Is the problem too massive and too deep, does it have too much momentum, for a Christian solution? It is not our purpose to argue that question thoroughly here. We assume rather that the racial crisis in its sociological aspects is a disease for which Christianity is a cure and that for some of the deep personal roots of that crisis Christianity, or a similarly God-centered religion, is the only cure. Jesus Christ did not come into the world to solve the race problem; that problem with the features it now has was unknown in the first century. But he did come to heal the estrangements of man from God, of man from man, and of the individual man from himself. In their worship of race and color, their divisiveness, their production of both vanity and humiliation, racial prejudice and discrimination are latter-day expressions of man's ancient evils: his idolatry, hatred, pride, greed, brutality. Classic Christianity holds that the God revealed to us in Jesus Christ has in his Son conquered these evils and can through his Holy Spirit overthrow their kingdoms whatever their form in any age. This assumption underlies all that is said here and dismisses the open or implied answer that Christianity is fundamentally inept and that we must therefore wait for the end of history or seek new dynamics and new strategies to resolve the racial conflict.

We have considered two of the easy, inadequate explanations of the white church's silence and inactivity in its relation to the Negro's struggle for his civil and social rights. We must note briefly two other quick and unsatisfactory answers to the question "Why doesn't the church do something about the race problem?" One of these answers encourages complacency; the other counsels despair. Neither tells us anything about the church we do not already know

and neither is a reliable index of what is happening or can happen
in the white church's approach to the racial crisis. The first of
these two answers states confidently that the church *is* doing something about the racial crisis. It points to the 1963 National Conference on Religion and Race, to the more than 200,000 people who
under religious and secular auspices gathered in Washington, D.C.,
August 28, 1963, for the March on Washington for Jobs and
Freedom, to the extraordinarily effective influence of the churches
in securing the passage of a strong civil rights bill by Congress in
1964. The defensive statement that the church is doing something
about the racial problem cites church resolutions on race which
demand creative action as well as changed attitudes; it summons as
witnesses the increasing number of white clergymen and laymen
who—obeying these resolutions—have desegregated their
churches, have joined Negroes in demonstrations, sit-ins, and
picket lines, and at great personal peril have helped Negroes regis-
ter to vote in Mississippi. This is all true and it is also true that in
numerous white churches Christians devoted to the Negro's cause
are discovering each other and for the first time in their churches'
histories are forming small discussion and action groups. These
references are no attempt to catalog all Christian activities in behalf of the Negro, rather they are samples of the proofs to which
defenders of Christians and their church can point with some justification to bolster their claim that white Christians do not abandon
the Negro entirely. But such proofs that white churches are identified with and involved in the Negro's quest for justice also prove
by their scarcity and by their speciality that the church at large is
not identified with or involved in the Negro's struggle. And the
indifference, inflexibility, and inactivity of the religious community
at large—the clergy and the laity—guarantee a worsening racial
conflict. Though we should applaud, encourage, and rejoice in
what the church is doing, the little it does thus far merely throws
into high relief the much it does not do. Everyone knows, to use
the title of Jackie Robinson's book, that "Baseball Has Done It"
—"it" meaning racial desegregation—and that the church has not
done it. Everyone knows the truth of the cliché which states that
11 o'clock on Sunday morning is the most segregated hour in
American life. But not everyone knows how crafty, intransigent,

and agile the white Christian can be in preventing those cultural and social changes which would release the Negro from residential, occupational, and psychological ghettos.

Those who do know how stubbornly white Christians resist the Negro's demand for justice find the fourth easy yet inadequate answer to the church's silence and inactivity not only tempting but sometimes overpowering. And that answer is that the white church is no longer the church, no longer God's gathered people, no longer "the body of Christ," no longer God's instrument in the world. Those who hold this view may not have rejected Christianity, may indeed be intensely devoted and obedient to it, but they have regretfully concluded that the church and Christianity, however close their former kinship, are now entirely unrelated. To such critics this cleavage between the church and Christianity is nowhere wider and more visible than in the white church's indifference to and abandonment of the Negro. Will D. Campbell, director of the Committee of Southern Churchmen, has in his little book, *Race and the Renewal of the Church*, asked, "How far can the church wander from its mission and nature and still remain the church? . . . An adherent of the free church tradition always hesitates to use the term 'heresy.' But what we have been saying is that racism has negated so much of the mission and nature of the church in America that there is no other name for it except that opprobrious term—heresy."[3] So, says Campbell, "We must ask ourselves, earnestly and prayerfully, whether *we* are still the church."[4]

When the gentle author of these hard words gave them and similar thoughts their first wide public utterance at the 1963 Conference on Religion and Race in Chicago, he was accused of making intemperate judgments and extravagant statements. But Campbell, a loyal churchman, was not so much launching a crusade against the church as he was regretfully noting an event—the accelerating departure of many humanitarian souls, white and Negro, from the institutional church to civil rights groups which have only a distant kinship with the church. He was noting what is now too

---

3. From RACE AND THE RENEWAL OF THE CHURCH by Will D. Campbell. Copyright © 1962, W. L. Jenkins. The Westminster Press. Used by permission. P. 13.
4. *Ibid.*, p. 9.

plain to ignore: While the greater part of the church tries to make up its mind as to whether the racial problem is its problem, the racial struggle passes the churches by and takes to the streets. While the white churches debate whether or not Martin Luther King, Jr., is a Christian, King's leadership of the Negro protest is challenged by Negro leaders who have contempt for the church and despise as weakness the Christian techniques King and his followers employ. The leadership of the Negro's crusade has not yet passed out of the hands of those Negro leaders who weigh the Negro's worth in Christian balances and fight his battles with Christian weapons. But there rises among frustrated and despairing Negroes and their white allies a new leadership which neither knows nor acknowledges the Christian evaluation of man and the Christian way to justice and equality. Is this the church? Is the church "out there where things are getting done for the Negro"?

There are Christians who answer Yes to this question. They do not say with Nietzsche that "God is dead and the churches are his tomb." Rather they say—more reverent toward God, less toward the church—that the churches are the tomb from which the living God has escaped into the world, that the real church has now abandoned its traditional form and appears in the shape of marches, pickets, demonstrations, and sit-ins. The obvious reply to this position distinguishes between saying that God is in such places and in such people—which we may well believe the truth—and saying that such places and people are the church—which is not the truth. Protestants who know their ecclesiastical traditions and doctrines are the first to say that the institutional, classically defined church is not a sacred precinct, that neither the building nor the people who call themselves Christians are God's house in any pre-emptive use of that title. On the contrary, Protestants who have a Protestant understanding of the nature of the church are more inclined to say with George Bernard Shaw, "Beware of the man whose God is in heaven." That is, beware of the man whose God is in any specific place. But to define the church as any place where God acts in human beings is to give the church so broad a definition that it loses all meaning. The church as God's gathered people includes sinners as well as saints, racists as well as men of goodwill. The church as a setting is that place where the word is truly preached and the sacraments faithfully administered. The sacraments have a social—a racial—significance; but their faithful administration allows for, though it does not condone, unfaithful participation. The church is still the church even though, faithful in some things, it is heretical in others.

What, then, are the answers to the question "Why doesn't the church do something about the racial problem?" We must seek answers which go beyond simple, facile, inadequate explanations, answers which will not only show us the church as we have not seen it before but also in the process reveal the ways in which the churches by responding to the racial challenge can themselves be redeemed and renewed. This becomes, then, inferentially, a book about the fall and the rise of the churches as that fall has occurred in Christians' abandonment of the Negro and as that rise can occur in their acceptance of the challenges put to them by the racial crisis. It becomes secondarily a defense of the Negro's quest for justice in society and acceptance by the whole church. For all their material affluence, the numerical strength of their membership, and their mood of complacent self-satisfaction, the white churches of the United States are as much in need of help as are humiliated and oppressed Negroes. And, ironically, that help is now available to white churches only through the people whom white Christians have for so long despised, rejected, and abandoned and through the crisis which white Christians fear or regret.

We shall not in the scope of this work be able to answer all of these questions, but they and a good many more need to be raised and answered. What, for example, is meant by laymen's increasing insistence that denominational resolutions on racial issues do not represent a consensus of lay churchmen? The line dividing racial opinion in the churches does not fall between laymen and clergymen, of course. The fact is that laymen disagree with each other on most social issues and especially on racial issues. Therefore few Protestant churches, if any—dependent as they are on the voice of their people—can speak unanimously about racial controversies. Racists and integrationists, conservatives and liberals, will in almost any local church prevent the development of a common mind on crucial social issues and will deaden the churches' will. Even a

small minority of vocal racists, particularly if their contributions to
the church are substantial, can usually stifle all declarations and
actions by the church in areas of racial conflict. We must therefore
add this factor—the paralyzing effect of sharp differences of opinion within local white churches. The democratic or representative
structure of most Protestant churches is a hindrance to social
action. Can this handicap be removed without destroying the local
church's basic democratic organization and without permanently
alienating one party or the other from the local church?

Again, the white church's withdrawal from the racial struggle is
to a considerable extent due to the erroneous ideas and attitudes
which many Christians hold toward ideological controversy and
social conflict. They view argument as disgraceful, conflict as un-
becoming to a Christian, and the use of force in the racial struggle
as a repudiation of the Prince of Peace. For some Christians these
views are merely ruses by which those who hold them escape from
their social responsibility. But for others such protestations are not
hypocritical, but on the contrary are sincere but misguided convictions which rise from a misunderstanding of the nature of Christian ethics and an unawareness of the legitimacy of some uses of
tension, conflict, and power. We therefore do well to ask to what
extent interpersonal tension and social conflict should be avoided
and how on the other hand they may be transformed from enemies
into allies. How do we explain many Christians' preference for
good taste over Christian duty? Why do they in meeting each other
and their neighbors pretend to have congenial racial views rather
than expose to each other their sharp differences? Why do they
prefer in their communities an unhealthful harmony which ignores
explosive racial tensions to an open, creative confrontation of the
problems? Why are there so many Christians who, belonging to the
same church, converse with each other only on the most superficial
level, smiling and amiable as they meet but never discussing with
each other the issues which trouble them most? We must answer
these questions, discovering why Christian communion is in most
churches a pretense, a cordial but uneasy fiction, rather than a
strengthening, creative reality.

What does the racial crisis and its challenge to white churches
tell us about the popular view of the nature of the church and the

role of the clergy? Questions about the irrelevancy of the church to
the Negro's struggle are at base questions about the nature of the
church, the faithfulness of its members, and the duties of its clergy.
Without exception, whenever the church contributes to the faults
of the age, it does so because it has forgotten what it is. The
church's part in creating and preserving the nation's racial shame
is only one of the types of amnesia which it has suffered in its long
history. But the symptoms of this amnesia, being current and
abundant, provide unique opportunities for a diagnosis of the
church's illness. The continuing exclusion of Negroes by white
churches and the detachment of the churches from the Negro's
plight and struggle are products of erroneous assumptions about
the character and purpose of the church. Eventually the nation's
racial crisis will compel most of the churches to re-examine the
central assumptions around which they are structured. Some local
churches and some denominations are already asking whether the
centers from which their life proceeds are biblically and doctrinally
whole. Do the racial sins of the church flourish like a fungus on the
surface of an institution which is healthy at its core or are they the
products of a general infection which originates in the deep, diseased centers of the church's life? Is the racial sickness of white
Christian churches social or theological in its inception?

The answers such questions seek introduce several additional
factors which contribute to the remoteness of the churches from
social problems and specifically from the racial problem. Even as
racial prejudice answers to no one name and as discrimination and
segregation cannot be explained by one definition, so too the
church's aloofness from the racial struggle rises from general and
minor as well as specific and major causes. Collectively these
minor generators of religious indifference to the Negro's burden
prove as destructive and as stubborn as any of the major causes.
What then are the sociological, historical, theological, ecclesiologi-
cal, and psychological imps which together hamper the church's
mission to society just as effectively as does any one of the principal devils? The principal explanations of the church's muteness
and paralysis in its relation to the racial problem are partial and
misleading if they are not accompanied by explorations of those
factors which contribute less directly to the estrangement of the

white churches from the Negro's quest for his rights as a man, a citizen, or a Christian. We must expose conditions both internal and external to the church, with which the church must cope in meeting the racial problem's challenge to its integrity and in reclaiming its own soul.

Finally, is there any hope for the church? It is now apparent that the racial justice in the United States can be achieved without the aid of the institutional church. The progress which the Negro has made in the past decade owes little credit to white-dominated institutional religion. It stems rather from the convergence of various political and economic forces which have been activated and focused by racial protests both within and outside the law. Much of the justice the Negro and his white allies have won through legislation and various forms of social protest has been obtained in spite of white Christians' opposition instead of through white Christians' daring, sacrificial support of the Negro's rights. To be fair, there are notable exceptions but the total picture is one in which white Christianity watches the Negro's crusade from the sidelines. The Negro moves forward nevertheless. So the crucial question now asks not whether the Negro will have the church's aid in his struggle for justice but whether the church, having so long ignored its duty to the Negro, can now survive as the church. Until recently in this country's history the church has been one of the decisive factors in the nation's approach to the Negro one-tenth of the population. As we shall see, the church's weight has usually been cast on the wrong side of the balances. Now, however, the church not only dwindles to a minor factor in the Negro's progress. By an ironic twist of history a reversal of roles makes the racial struggle the decisive test of the church's integrity. In its massiveness and its penetration of the church's vital centers, the racial struggle threatens and challenges the church as does nothing else. So the racial problem becomes decisive for the church, compelling the church either to default and cease to be the church or to find in the threat and challenge confronting it the occasion for a radical renewal and reformation.

2

History of a White Quandary

This book is a diagnostic rather than a historical approach to the interplay of Negroes and white Christians. Its theme, however, rests on certain historical events and trends which must be briefly cited. Although we do not need to retell here a history which has been many times well told, we do need to see the white man's conflicting feelings and contradictory actions in his dealings with the Negro; and we need to see these shifting and antithetical patterns in their historical development in the official actions of churches and in the lives of individual Christians. We shall then be able to ask in what measure Christian churches in mid-twentieth century perpetuate the unstable moods and indecisive conduct which were the typical mind and behavior of churches and Christians in the earlier American centuries of racial encounter. Covert racial discrimination and oppression in the twentieth century have their antecedents in the overtly expressed prejudices and exploitations of early centuries. The current phenomenon camouflages itself in subtleties which were not considered necessary in the white man's earlier oppression of the Negro. As a visit to a psychopathic hospital helps the perceptive person understand the peculiarities of normal human behavior, so a brief return to the times of our boldly open oppression of the Negro and to the days when Christian efforts to rationalize slavery were crass and undisguised will help us understand the present-day inconsistencies of white Christians in their relation to Negroes.

To say that in its total sweep the relation of white Christian churches to Negroes has been marked by unbroken indifference and brutal betrayal may make useful propaganda but it is poor history. The facts do include eras in which Christians callously neglected the religious life of Negroes. The seventeenth century was primarily such an era. The prevailing attitude among the planters during this time was expressed as the era closed by a writer in John Dunton's *Athenian Oracle* issued in London in 1705: "Talk to a planter of the soul of a Negro, and he'll be apt to tell you (or at least his actions speak loudly) that the body of one of them may be worth twenty pounds; but the soul of an hundred of them would not yield him one farthing."[1] All slaveholders were not members of Christian churches but many of them were, and those that were tended to view the Negro first as chattel and commodity and only secondly, if at all, as a spiritual being.

But this period was followed, and in its closing years overlapped, by one in which some attention was shown to the spiritual life of Negroes. Noteworthy was the work of the Society for the Propagation of the Gospel in Foreign Parts, founded in 1701 by the Anglican Church for the pastoral care of British emigrants and soldiers, officials and merchants. Within a few years after this society's birth its missionaries included American Indians and Negroes among their converts, and the missionaries deserve credit for a conscientious effort to Christianize Negro slaves. The missionaries were caught, however, as were many other Christians then and later, in an ironic conflict of interests. To increase the range of their evangelism and make it include Indians and Negroes, the missionaries felt compelled to restrict or to deny altogether Christianity's social and political implications. It became expedient for them to deny outright the original Christian concept that it is illegal for Christians to enslave converted and baptized Negroes, lest such doctrine and its threat to planters prove a hindrance to the evangelizing of the Negro. Whatever the limitations of their view of the Negro, however tangled their motives, these missionaries were not indifferent to the spiritual welfare of bound as well as free Negroes.

The devotion, tact, and perseverance of the Society's missionaries as well as the intellectual and spiritual responsiveness of

---

1. From the NEGRO IN VIRGINIA, © 1940, Compiled by Workers of the Writers Program of the Work Projects Administration, reprinted by permission of Hastings House, Publishers, Inc. P. 98.

slaves are attested by one of John S. Bassett's quotations from the *Colonial Records*: "Mr. Taylor in speaking in 1716 about the Duckinfield slaves, intimates that all the efforts made to convert them were made by himself. His own method of proceeding with the negro converts he recounts as follows: 'I hope I took a method with the negro young man and the mustee young woman, whom I baptized, which will please the Society, which was this: I made them get our church catechism perfectly without book, and then I took some pains with them to make them understand it, and especially the baptismal covenant, and to persuade them, faithfully and constantly to perform the great things they were to promise at their baptism, and ever after to perform to God; and then I caused them to say the catechism one Lord's Day and the other another Lord's Day before a large congregation, which they did both distinctly and so perfectly that all that heard them admired their saying it so well, and with great satisfaction to myself I baptized these two persons.' "[2]

Another period in which white Christians showed a general indifference to the spiritual as well as the physical lot of Negroes was the 49 years from 1865 to 1914. In his pamphlet "The Ecumenical Movement and the Racial Problem," W. A. Visser 't Hooft, general secretary of the World Council of Churches, referred to this period as the silent era, a time in which even those churches which had vociferously championed the abolition of slavery largely ignored the racial problems gathering during these years and turned their backs on the liberated slaves. (It is not coincidental that this was also the era of a vigorously expanded Protestant foreign mission program—a possible compensation abroad for a glaring default at home.) In this era the North, preoccupied with its rapid industrial development, not only neglected the Negro it had freed and left him to flounder but also in a nationwide political maneuver returned the Negro to the control of his former master and to a condition little better than his previous slavery. The silent churches tacitly and passively complied with the national mood. Many of the evils which haunt race relations today arose not in slave days but in the early years of that period in which the North

---

2. John S. Bassett, *Slavery and Servitude in North Carolina*, Johns Hopkins University Studies, Volume XIV, Baltimore, 1896 (Colonial Records, II, p. 332).

betrayed the man it had freed, "selling" the Negro once more to the South to discharge a burden and to gain political leverage.

Even so, the anti-slavery movement did find its most vocal, consistent, and courageous champions in the church during the years immediately preceding the Civil War. Not only was anti-slavery, as the historian Henry Wilson put it, the child of Christian faith; it was also the consuming objective of a small, unrelenting, tireless minority within the church. Their influence and their success are best measured by the fact that they rather than the political abolitionists received the full measure of the South's hatred and contempt. We may well ask which was the church in the days leading to the freeing of the Negroes—the small band of Christian abolitionists who forced the issue or the vast masses of people who bore the name of Christian but were silent and indifferent. In any event we cannot say that the silent era gives us the only true picture of the church against the racial backdrop. Such a sweeping dismissal of the church simply will not bear the weight of the facts.

We must acknowledge also that the churches, sometimes indifferent, were also sometimes cruel in their treatment of Negroes. Aside from the known physical brutality of individual slaveowners who considered themselves Christian, the churches as institutions and their official representatives expressed toward and about Negroes barbaric attitudes which caused the Negroes deep spiritual wounds. Juan Comas, professor of anthropology at the Mexican School of Anthropology, noted how in three separate centuries Christian ministers sought to prove a divinely ordained inferiority of Negroes to white men: "For instance, in 1772 the Reverend Thomas Thompson published a monogram, 'The trade in Negro slaves on the African coast in accordance with humane principles and with the laws of revealed religion,' in 1852 the Rev. Josiah Priest published 'A defense of slavery,' while C. Carroll (1900) in his work 'The Negro as a beast or in the image of God' includes a chapter ('Biblical and Scientific Proofs that the Negro is not a Member of the Human Race') in which he asserts that 'all scientific research confirms his [the Negro's] typically simian nature.' "[3] Such distortions of Christianity and of the Bible to produce a moral defense for slavery were not rare but, on the con-

3. Juan Comas, *Racial Myths* (Paris: UNESCO, 1951), pp. 20–21.

trary, constituted an extensive literature in the slavery era. The debasement of the Negro by white Christians was never more vicious than when it appealed to doctrine and the Bible for its support. Guion Griffis Johnson summarized the Christians' mood as it appeared in North Carolina in the following way: "At first favorable to the gradual emancipation of slavery, the churches came to look upon slavery as a justifiable evil and diligently searched the Scriptures to find a defense for their position."[4] John Hope Franklin shows how the appeal to Scripture to remove the guilt of slavery developed in the churches' fluctuating mood into the use of religion in praise of slavery: "Gradually the doctrine that freedom was inherent in Christianity began to wane in popularity and was supplanted by a point of view that was in itself a rationalization of the institution. This view was that slavery was good in that it brought heathens into contact with Christianity and led to the salvation of their souls."[5]

However, there can be no questioning the existence of another mood in the white churches, a different understanding of the Scriptures, and a contrasting view of the nature of the Negro as a man. In a study of slavery and servitude in North Carolina John S. Bassett quoted an instructive account from Biggs's *History of the Kehukee Baptist Association*. In 1783 this association of North Carolina Baptists in reply to a question about "the duty of a master toward his slave who refused to attend family worship" concluded that "It is the duty of every master of a family to give his slaves liberty to attend the worship of God *in his family,* and likewise it is his duty to exhort them to it, and to endeavor to convince them of their duty; and then to leave them to their own choice."[6] This simple decision by these Baptists exhibits a concern for the spiritual life of the Negro plus a wholesome respect for his freedom of conscience. They were not willing to free the Negro's body but neither did they try either to deny or to coerce his soul.

From an abundant history we could continue to draw such contrasting illustrations indefinitely. These are enough to show that no

---

4. Guion Griffis Johnson, *Ante-Bellum North Carolina* (Chapel Hill: The University of North Carolina Press, 1937), p. 467.
5. John Hope Franklin, *From Slavery to Freedom* (New York: Alfred A. Knopf, © 1948), pp. 85–86.
6. Bassett, *op. cit.,* pp. 55–56.

one mood and no one behavior defines the whole position of white Christian churches in their relation to Negroes. If the history of white Christians and Negroes were set down geometrically, it would describe a curious, jumbled pattern of broken, jagged, criss-crossing lines. The pattern would be totally lacking in symmetrical forms, straight lines, and graceful consistencies. This says analogi-cally that in its total course the relation of white Christian churches to Negroes has been marked not so much by indifference, cruel neglect, and brutal betrayal as it has by ambivalence and vacillation. Ambivalence, because white Christians have held and have been moved by alternate and simultaneous emotions of at-traction to and revulsion from Negroes—love and hatred, the will to help and the willingness to hinder, tenderness and brutality. Vacillation, because the conduct of white Christians in their en-counter with Negroes has swung like their mood from one pole to the other. The white man's racial behavior has in its curious and contradictory patterns reflected his tangled, conflicting emotions. The true picture of white churches and American Negroes requires clashing, angular lines which depict the white man's puzzling emo-tional duality in his relation to the Negro and the devious course of his churches in their move toward and their flight from the Negro.

The white man's quandary is old. It began with the almost simultaneous settlement of whites and Negroes in continental North America. The historical fact—the coming of 20 Negroes to Jamestown, Virginia, in 1619 on a Dutch frigate 12 years after the arrival of the first white man and a year before the coming of the first white woman—has spawned many myths. But we know in fact that these Negroes were not slaves but indentured servants—a classification under which many white men were to follow Negroes to this land. There is strong evidence that these legally and temporarily bound Negro apprentices were baptized Christians who were on their way to the new land through Spain and Portugal and that in the course of piracy or trade they had been transferred to the Dutch frigate from a Spanish war vessel. "The conversion of Negroes began before the first shipload reached Virginia. The Spanish names indicate that a number of the first Africans had already been baptized. Early mention was also made of William Tucker, baptized at Jamestown in 1624, and of John Graweer who, in 1641, bought a young boy from Lieutenant Sheppard so that he could 'bring him up in the fear of God.' It has been estimated that as many as 1,000 Negroes followed William Tucker, the first native-born Afro-American, to the font at Jamestown for baptism."[7] Whatever the fictions that sprouted from the root fact that the Negroes came—or, better, were brought—to Jamestown, two facts are demonstrable: the Negroes were subservient and they were Christians. The dual status of the Negroes—preserved when slavery superseded indenture—established in the white man's soul a duality, a contradiction, which continues to haunt the white man and harass the Negro three and a half centuries later.

Though the first Negroes in Virginia were indentured servants and could secure and in some cases did secure their freedom by working for it or buying it, they aroused in the white Virginians, who were not ignorant of the Spanish and Portuguese slave trade, the hope that the Negro might be the answer to their desire for cheap labor and relief from drudgery. The white man had dreamed —as had men of other races—that he would one day discover a creature intermediate between man and animal—strong, rational but soulless—which could relieve the white man of all toil and let him live the genteel, leisurely, conscience-free life for which he believed himself created. The Czechoslovakian writer Karel Capek dramatized this dream in his play *R. U. R.*, which presents brute, efficient, insensitive, artificially created persons doing the work of man. The Virginians thought that in the Negro they had found such a creature—tractable, tireless, divinely created to serve men of lighter skin. So they enslaved the Negro, made him a robot, and began, slowly at first, to import more and more Negro slaves.

Some white men not only hoped that the Negro would be their robot; they also did all they could to debase the Negro and make their hope come true. When some years later Negro preachers used the Bible as a guide to freedom, the Virginia legislature prohibited the preaching of the gospel by Negroes and mulattoes. One of the legislators, Henry Berry, complimented the general assembly for this action in words which revealed the white man's determination to destroy the Negro as a person. He admitted that Virginia had "closed every avenue by which light may enter slaves' minds. If we

7. *Negro in Virginia, op. cit.,* pp. 96–98.

could extinguish the capacity to see the light, our work would be completed; they would then be on a level with the beasts of the field and we should be safe."[8] We have here not only a refreshingly honest confession but also the starkly naked picture of one man's resolve to bestialize another solely for material gain.

In seeking this kind of advantage and this kind of safety the white man encountered resistance in the Negro. Proofs that Negroes as a people did not accept the white man's mythical descriptions of the Negro as a willing slave who through slavery fulfilled his nature and his destiny are evident in the steps which the white man had to take to maintain ownership and control of his human property. To be sure there were many Negroes who for a variety of reasons conformed to the picture thrust upon them by their masters. Awakening to self-consciousness in a slave system, cut off by ignorance from any denial that things had always been thus for the Negro and always would be, confronted by a strategically positioned, numerically superior, and powerfully armed master, many Negroes either surrendered to the system in apathy and despair or protested against it in ways which annoyed the slaveowners but did not threaten their dominance. But there were enough rebellions to convince the white masters that their robots were human after all and might therefore become ungovernable, might indeed like Capek's automatons develop their intelligence and express their spirit of revolt. And, paradoxically, the white man aided the Negro's developing knowledge, encouraged in the Negro an awareness of his own innate dignity, and spurred his rebellious spirit to action by giving him the Bible and teaching him to read it—for the master-slave principle a fatal mistake.

Moreover the white man's search for a robot met opposition among the members of his own race and within himself. Proofs that the white man never fully accepted his own fictional descriptions of the Negro's nature are evident in the number of myths to which he appealed and which he invented to support what he wanted to believe about his slave. To ease the pestering suspicion that his evaluation of the Negro might be false and his treatment of the Negro evil, the white man summoned anthropological, philosophical, creedal, and biblical arguments to his defense. Being a

---

8. *Ibid.*, p. 105.

child of English jurisprudence and a Christian of sorts, the slave-owner needed a rationale for his exploitation of the Negro. So he appealed to the slavery-sanctioning views of Greek philosophers, Roman law, and the Patristic writers of early Christianity. He cited psuedo-anthropological proofs of the physical and mental inferiority of the Negro, ecclesiastical edicts authorizing the capture and use of inferior peoples, biblical texts which could be distorted to put the blame for slavery on God. For the 246 years of American slavery white American Christians, with some notable exceptions, were pestered by the breach between a definition of the Negro which made slavery defensible and a personal knowledge of the Negro which make slavery indefensible, between their lust for the economic benefits of slavery and their inescapable gospel about God's love for all men. They collided with themselves as in their souls, moved at once by human revulsion and human sympathy, they ran toward and away from the Negro. This rent in the white man's mind and soul could never be healed so long as the white man insisted on retaining his civil and Christian values and at the same time a slave system which rested on a patently false view of the Negro as subhuman. Nor can this wound be healed in the twentieth century so long as the white man clings to his civil and religious values with one hand and rudely dismisses the Negro as an inherently secondary being with the other. This is the essence of the white man's ambivalence and vacillation toward the Negro. The white Christian wanted several incompatible things in one: his fine sense of English justice and approval for his oppression of a fellow human being, a warm personal relationship to the Negro and complete control over the Negro, the Negro as a human being and as a robot, faithfulness to the command to take the gospel to all men and assurance that the gospel would not spoil his slave. It can be concluded from this that all the racial turmoil has not been between the races; much of it has been within the soul of the white Christian.

How did the white Christian try to handle and resolve the tensions created in him and in his church by his incompatible views of slavery and of Christian values? For some Christians the resolution was simple: it required merely the release of one horn of the dilemma or the other, the surrender of human capital or the rejec-

tion of Christian morality. John Woolman, the Quaker, was unquestionably the prototype of those few Christians who escaped
both guilt and spiritual turmoil by repudiating all arguments for
the oppression of the Negro and who through their simple, gentle,
yet audacious lives gave freedom to the slave as they could and
dignity where freedom was not theirs to give. Other Christians
found an equally simple solution of the perplexity produced by the
collision of slavery and Christian principles. George Whitefield,
English evangelist and yoke-fellow of John Wesley, settled the
slave question on the basis of expediency. Breaking with Wesley,
who abhorred slavery, Whitefield said after visiting Georgia: "To
locate people in Georgia on such a footing [in a hot country
without slaves to serve them] is little better than tying their legs
and bidding them walk."[9] The evangelist practiced what he
preached. He became the owner of a 640 acre plantation and
several slaves, using his profits to help finance his orphanage at
Bethesda, Georgia. He, too, had his disciples, Christians who practiced slavery without compunction, apparently wholly unaware of
any conflict between the faith they professed and the dehumanizing
slavery they employed or approved.

But in the slavery era the great mass of Christians fluctuated
uneasily between the two extremes, finding for themselves neither
the peace of Woolman's "inner stillness" nor Whitefield's crass
insensibility. These Christians—the spiritual progenitors of most
twentieth-century American white Christians—temporized, postponed, vacillated, suffered the emotional and mental torments of
their indecisiveness, projected their unidentified irritation onto the
Negro in unpredictable acts of hostility and indulgence, driving the
slave with the lash by day and watching by his sickbed at night.
White Christians' vacillations produced in the Old South a hodge-
podge of good and evil, tenderness and cruelty, affection and contempt, toughness and laxity—a mixture which permits the preju-
diced historian to draw from selected illustrations whatever conclusions about the church and race he desires to portray. But the
true picture of white Christians is one of inconstancy and contradictions, a spotty picture erratically streaked with light and dark-

9. Ralph Betts Flanders, *Plantation Slavery in Georgia* (Chapel Hill: The University
of North Carolina Press, 1933), p. 16.

ness. From the beginning of slavery to our own time the relation of white Christians to Negroes has been one of ambivalence and vacillation.

What were some of the effects of such contradictions on Christianity, on the faith itself? Inevitably Christianity was distorted by the uses to which its professors put it. Christianity's career in the history of Negro-white relations has been the story of ideological contortion as Christians twisted and turned it in a never quite successful effort to reconcile the ethics of their faith and the profits of human exploitation. We have already noted how in the seventeenth century, when the white man was pestered by the thought that baptized Christians could not legally be held in bondage, Christianity's threat to the slave system was removed by a series of colonial measures. These measures reduced Christianity to an irrelevant sentiment by declaring that the profession of the Christian religion does not change a man's civil estate and that therefore baptized Negroes could be legally held in slavery. The white man thus kept his lucrative system and his sense of faithfulness to the gospel's demand that it could be preached evangelistically to every creature. But he could achieve this accommodation only by debasing and departmentalizing his religion.

Having eliminated Christianity as a threat to the exploitation of the Negroes, the white man did not find it difficult to indulge in an even more flagrant duplicity and turn Christianity into slavery's partner. I have elsewhere shown at some length how Christianity was converted by Christians into a defender and ally of exploitation.[10] With amazing adroitness the white man appealed to Christianity as proof of his innate superiority over the Negro and as a justification for the oppression of Negroes and at the same time gave liberal doses of a partial Christian gospel to Negroes in order to make them more tractable. We find a striking illustration of this perfidy in a booklet, *The Spirit of Christmas at Monticello,* in which Julian P. Boyd mentions the white planters' use of Christmas as a soporific to lull slaves into contentment with slavery: "Most [of the slaves] celebrated by singing and dancing, but a few indubitably looked inward to ponder their condition and to wonder

---

10. Kyle Haselden, *The Racial Problem in Christian Perspective* (New York: Harper and Row, 1959), pp. 34–60.

why it was in the power of some to grant freedom and to limit the grant to the days of Christmas. By the nineteenth century one of those who had so pondered [Frederick Douglass] described this respite as a calculated means for keeping down the spirit of the slaves, a season in which drinking and carousing in the quarters was not only permitted but encouraged, a season in which the slave was cheated 'with a dose of vicious dissipation, artfully labelled with the name of liberty,' with the result that after a season of dissipation many were led to think there was little to choose between liberty and slavery."[11] This use of Christmas to pacify Negro slaves is a specific illustration of the general perversion of Christianity as a partner of slavery.

The deputizing of Christianity as a partner of racial oppression was part of the white man's search for what W. J. Cash in *The Mind of the South* called "the savage ideal . . . that ideal whereunder dissent and variety are completely suppressed and men become, in all their attitudes, professions, and actions, virtual replicas of one another."[12] The southern white man never quite achieved the total isolation in which he sought to wrap his abuse of a whole race; but by exiling native prophets, equating criticism with treachery, and making God his partner in the exploitation of the Negro the white man became increasingly agile and active in warding off all moral and civil blows struck for the freeing of the Negro.

Mississippi and Alabama remain today as potent illustrations of the closed mind and the closed society which once gripped most of the South and scattered localities throughout the whole country. In these states the native white dissenter is branded a traitor and driven out. For example, Charles Morgan, Jr., the young Birmingham, Alabama, lawyer who protested the bombing of a Negro church and the murder of four Negro Sunday school pupils was in 1963 forced to flee from Birmingham and settle eventually in Atlanta, Georgia. The visitor from outside—though he come to help the Negro and not necessarily to rebuke the white man—does

11. Julian P. Boyd, *The Spirit of Christmas at Monticello* (New York: Oxford University Press, 1964), p. 38.
12. W. J. Cash, *The Mind of the South*, Doubleday Anchor Books (Garden City, N.Y.: Doubleday and Company, Inc.) (Copyright 1941, by Alfred A. Knopf, Inc.), p. 101.

so at great risk to his life. In 1964 three out-of-state civil rights workers were murdered in Mississippi. Though the Federal Bureau of Investigation charged 21 Mississippi men with the abuse of the workers' rights (not being empowered to charge the Mississippians with murder), it is still unlikely that they will be found guilty by a Mississippi jury, whatever the evidence. Many Negroes have been killed by white Mississippians, but no Mississippi jury has ever found a white man guilty of first-degree murder where the victim was a Negro. And in these states even Christian preaching against racial injustice is intimidated. Now and then a minister dares condemn his people's involvement in a wicked system of racial oppression. But if he is explicit and unequivocating in his condemnation of local customs he might as well have an eye open for another charge. It will not be long before he needs it. In Western culture the closed society, "the savage ideal," is approximated only where Christian judgment against the individual and his total society is silenced—Hitler's Germany, Stalin's Russia, South Africa, and the deep South in the United States.

Inevitably the white man's abuse of the Christian faith defiled the faith itself. In at least three respects white Christianity became heretical under the tortures to which it was subjected by the white Christian's ambivalence and vacillation. First, its ethical content was degraded. A rationalized racial injustice did to Christianity what the savage did to the dog—tamed the enemy and made it an ally. Eventually, under continuous domestication, the dog's freedom and self-dependence—its nature—was changed. When Christianity was eliminated as a threat to systematic oppression of the Negro and by a cunning sorcery transformed into a defense of that oppression, its nature was sullied. Its judgmental vigor and its redemptive power as a social conditioner were destroyed. Except for its catechism of private virtues the ethical content of Christianity was emptied by the deliberate exemption of the largest area of social injustice from the Christian definition of good and evil. Since the moral nerve of a religion atrophies when it is no longer permitted to function, ethical Christianity disappeared. It was supplanted by a code of manners and private moralities and by an otherworldly theology which not only could ignore the plight of the abused Negro but which could also justify that oppression. It is not

accidental that today the region of the country in which the defense of slavery blunted the judgmental edge of the Christian faith
—the South—remains the one most impervious to the social imperatives of Christian ethics. There has been throughout the
United States a traditional opposition to the social applications of
the Christian gospel, but nowhere is that opposition so recalcitrant
and so passionate as it is in those areas where social ethics
threaten the profitable oppression of a whole race. In the South
and in border states inhuman practices produced deficient Christian doctrines. More than a hundred years ago the great Anglican
preacher Frederick W. Robertson understood how practices fabricate dogmas. In his renowned sermon "Obedience the Organ of
Spiritual Knowledge," he wrote: "Again, slavery is defended
philosophically by some. The Negro on his skull and skeleton, they
say, has God's intention of his servitude written: he is the inferior
animal therefore it is right to enslave him. Did this doctrine precede the slave trade? Did man arrive at it, and then in consequence
conscientiously proceed with human traffic? Or was it invented to
defend a practice existing already—the offspring of self-interest?
Did not men first make slaves, and then search about for reasons to make their conduct plausible to themselves?"[13] So the
defenders of slavery—and after them the defenders of discrimination and segregation—invented an ethic-less gospel so that their
conduct might become plausible to themselves and invulnerable to
the attacks of the world.

Second, the white man's endeavor to preserve his religion and
yet make it serve his basest interest not only eliminated the hard
judgmental imperatives of the faith but also exaggerated the sentimental, individualistic, devotional ingredients of the faith. The
religion extruded by the pressures of the white man's religious
duality was one from which the rigorous virtues of truth and justice were squeezed out and in which the warm, tender, lesser
merits of church-going, Bible-reading, courtesy, and hospitality
remained. The essential balance was disturbed and the resulting
heresy, a partial Christianity, enabled the white man to think himself highly religious—as in part he was—even though his religion
was entirely cut off from his most vicious social sin. His evange-

---

13. Frederick W. Robertson, *Sermons* (New York: Harper & Brothers, 1870), p. 303.

listic and missionary fervor, his faithfulness to his mechanical and
ritualistic religious acts, his sentimentalities—these gave him a
warm glow of personal righteousness; but his religious imbalance
made him increasingly insensitive to his personal involvement in
the most cruel social evil of his day.

This does not mean that all of the abnormal developments in the
white man's religion were deliberate camouflages for his racial
injustice, that his religion became merely a deceptive mask. It
requires a narrow and arbitrary definition of religion to dismiss
him as in no sense a Christian. His religion was genuinely held,
served, and propagated. It means only that the part of his religion
which survived the assaults of his economy experienced a com-
pensatory growth, as one lung grows stronger when the other has
been collapsed or removed. This is the nature of heresies: Their
cherished singularity grows more and more pronounced and the
heretic's pride in his faith's peculiar emphasis becomes more and
more inordinate. The religion with which the white man countered
attacks on slavery and subsequent racial oppressions evolved into
that kind of heresy—partial, extreme, and proud.

Third, it was not enough for the white man to tame his religion
into a defender of his racial systems and to conceal its ethical
emptiness under magnified and extravagant manners. Having
erected these two religious walls around his oppression of the
Negro, he had to throw about them a further defense—anti-intellectualism—lest biblical criticism, emerging social and scientific
studies, and new theological theories crash his religious defenses of
racial injustice. This anti-intellectualism required the expulsion of
home-grown prophets who dared question the rational or the biblical arguments for slavery and segregation. The South has had no
lack of brilliant, questioning minds and dissenting spirits who as
prophets without honor, as rebels against a rebellious cause, risked
honor, fortune, and life in their personal attacks on the South's
decadent, closed systems. But the tragedy of the South has been
compounded by its diligent expulsion of native dissenters. This
disgorging process, which began early in the region's history, produced a heavy exodus which continues in mid-twentieth century.
Anti-intellectualism required also the exclusion of alien ideas.
Again, it is no coincidence that the South and the border states

were more persistent and more successful than any other part of the country in resisting the ecumenical movement, evolutionary theories, the social gospel, biblical criticism, and new theological currents. Each of these developments was a direct or indirect threat to a social structure which imprisoned the Negro at a second-class level. All windows and doors had to be shut and barred against the winds of change, for change in any area of southern life threatened to upset the South's basic social pattern. Native prophets continued to arise and change seeped through, but anti-intellectualism remains the mood of that part of the United States which has been traditionally committed to the subjugation of the Negro.

Undoubtedly the great substream of southern anti-intellectualism was fed by many springs, but unquestionably also—as Thomas D. Clark illustrates in his contribution to *Change in the Contemporary South*—the principal spring was the South's preoccupation with threats to its racial forms. Clark notes that the anti-intellectual "strand is most evident in controversies sparked by opinion on the race issue."[14] He cites how some southern communities "prune public library shelves of all books, including children's pre-school books, which remotely might be construed to bear on race relations and to imply support for racial integration."[15] In 1956, Clark reminds us, South Carolina House Resolution 2289 requested "the State Library Board to remove from circulation certain books antagonistic and inimical to the traditions of South Carolina and further request that said Library Board screen more carefully certain publications before circulating same."[16] There is solid ground for the conclusion that though many factors caused the South to turn its back on its own scholars and repudiate those who from the outside tempted the South to rebel against its thought patterns, its anti-intellectualism was primarily the product of a southern determination to preserve forever its bi-level racial structure.

Although the whole society had a stake in the suppression of ideas which threatened the southern way of life and although many

---

14. *Change in the Contemporary South*, edited by Allan P. Sindler (Durham, N.C.: Duke University Press, 1963), p. 13.
15. *Ibid.*, pp. 13–14.
16. *Ibid.*, footnote 25, p. 24.

of the social parts—including the schools—contributed to this mentality, the church carried the burden of it. To the church the people entrusted final refutation of all arguments which assaulted the bastions of slavery and segregation. The ultimate defense was the religious defense and it is no strange consequence that the white church became and remained the stronghold of these two interacting, coeval mentalities—race prejudice and anti-intellectualism. It may be true, as Kenneth K. Bailey states, that the South's all-pervading poverty shaped southern religious ethos more than ecclesiastical independence and racial segregation.[17] But it is worth noting that the South's economic rise has not been paralleled by the disappearance of segregation and by the decline of suspicion of changing ideas and events in the life of the church.

It is in the white-Negro encounter in the South that we see most clearly the development of the white quandary—ambivalence and vacillation—and that quandary's products: a religion deprived of its judgmental vigor, reduced to its sentimental ingredients, and anti-intellectual in mood and mentality. But this is not to suggest that this dilemma and its derivatives are uniquely southern. What we have seen in the South appears in various forms wherever in the country the racial problem intensifies. Historically the white man's ambivalence in his relation to the Negro has not been so pronounced in the North as in the South. Except in the big cities there was little physical proximity between the races and the northern white man was in general never so strongly attracted to or repelled by the Negro as the southern white man. But his vacillation was more abrupt, less personal, less disturbing to the individual conscience. The northern churches' concern for the Negro reached a peak in the Civil War and pre-Civil War days, fanned and goaded by the abolitionists. From that high point white Christian concern for the Negro dipped sharply in the late 1880's, was almost entirely dormant during the late stages of the Social Gospel era, and did not begin to rise until World War I. Not until the 1930's did numerically major denominations in the North specifically and officially condemn all forms of racial segregation, and it was 1946 before the Federal Council of the Church of Christ (now the Na-

---

17. Kenneth K. Bailey, *Southern White Protestantism in the Twentieth Century* (New York: Harper and Row, 1964), p. 7.

tional Council) renounced segregation as a violation of the Christian gospel. Until the close of World War I and the first massive migration of Negroes northward, the Negro exerted little direct pressure on northern churches and, except for missionary forays among southern Negroes and the building of Negro schools in the South, these churches had a detached, theoretical approach to the Negroes' problems. Following World War I and even more so after World War II, the white churches in the northern cities found the Negro and his problems on their doorsteps. Theoretical concern turned quickly into feigned apathy and in many cases into open hostility. Ambivalence and vacillation—though their forms, intensities, and products vary from one part of the country to the other —epitomize and characterize the white Christian's relation to his Negro brother. The social patterns which racial pressures developed in the South have with variations emerged in northern communities where racial tensions have flared. And the psychological defenses of segregation perfected in the South have proved irresistibly tempting to northern white Christians confronted by increasing racial conflict. As we now look more directly at the current scene, we shall discover that the racial mood and mentality which developed over many years in the South are now, with insignificant exception, the nationwide character of Christian churches confronted by the racial problem.

3

The Quandary's Current Crisis

It is said that some of the more primitive Indian tribes in the United States lived at one site until the accumulated debris made further habitation of that area unpleasant if not impossible. At that point the tribe, leaving its rubbish behind, moved to another site and started all over again. Fortunately or unfortunately the church is incapable of detaching itself from its past. It cannot start all over again. On the contrary, it carries great loads of debris from its yesteryears into its tomorrows, occasionally dropping some of its trash—and sometimes losing its treasure—as it moves from one generation to another.

In the history of its relation to the Negro the white church accumulated and brought forward into its present life few achievements and much hampering debris. We are not concerned here with ascribing guilt by inheritance. On the face of it, it is unjust— as well as impracticable—to require twentieth-century white people to recompense twentieth-century Negroes for abuses whites heaped upon Negroes 200 years ago. (Negroes will do well to collect what contemporary whites owe them.) But though it is patently false as well as unfair to blame present generations of white Christians for the racial sins of their fathers, it remains true that "the fathers have eaten sour grapes and the children's teeth are set on edge." For what does concern us as we consider the church's unbroken continuity is that Christians today inherit racial mind-sets and ecclesiastical patterns which burden the present with the bigotries and the crippling social structures developed in the past. Though some Christians achieve a modest success in their effort to escape this racial burden, most Christians live

on top of accumulated racial debris and are not free to pull up
stakes and move elsewhere. The dual and contradictory moods and
mentalities which white Christians perfected through 350 years of
relationships with Negroes still govern white churches.

Indeed, the white man's racial quandary—the mixed emotions
which draw him to and drive him away from the Negro—reaches a
crisis in the sixth decade of the twentieth century as the Negro
demands that the white man translate his Christian professions
into concrete practices. The church, confronted by a challenge it
cannot ignore, must join the struggle for racial justice, stand aside
and die, or oppose the struggle and be crushed by the avalanche
of rapidly changing racial patterns and moods. An increasing
number of white clergymen and a much smaller proportion of
laymen have elected to join the crusade against racial oppression.
At the other extreme some churches have become the willing tools
of white obstructionists who are determined to defend to the last
ditch white supremacy and the right of the white man to keep the
Negro subservient. But by and large the church stands midway
between these two positions—dazed, uncertain, and inactive—
while the time in which it can make a free decision swiftly passes.

Nowhere and at no time have white Christian ambivalence and
vacillation been more evident and more pathetic than in the United
States churches in the twentieth century. They face massive surges
of racial upheaval with paralyzed indecision and immobility. The
Christian people in all but a few churches view the racial decisions
and directives of their national officers with suspicion and make no
effort to implement those directives on the local scene. They listen
to their minister's vague, sweet words about love and brotherhood
with a conscience-lulling consent, but they oppose all efforts to
translate these beautiful generalities into a desegregated community. They read—or, at least, occasionally hear read—biblical
words which can only be fulfilled in a racially open society, but
they trust the wisdom of reactionary realtors more than that of the
Bible in this world's affairs. They bask in theoretical love but fear
implemented justice. They accept the arguments for racial righteousness but despise and fear the acts which can secure racial
justice.

Thus the ambivalent, vacillating church becomes in our present society a hindrance rather than an aid to social progress and to a resolving of the racial problem. An interesting example of the extremes to which the church will go in protecting the segregated system with which it has identified itself occurred recently in South Carolina. In 1964 the board of trustees of Furman University—a Southern Baptist college in Greenville, South Carolina—voted to integrate the student body. The South Carolina Baptist Convention refused to approve the trustees' integration decision. They did so despite the fact that a segregated university is automatically by-passed by many foundations willing to aid needful colleges and despite the fact that under the Civil Rights Act schools must desegrate to qualify for federal aid. Here the church blocks the efforts of one of its schools to move with the social trends of the day. It is willing to pay a high price financially to preserve the racial patterns with which it is identified. Subsequently Furman University admitted a Negro student despite the objection of the Baptist Convention.

In other parts of the country the church's efforts to block progress in race relations is a more subtle combination of laudable pretensions and performances which refute those pretensions. Much is heard today about Communist front organizations and about clergymen who are deceived into and betrayed by such groups. The tellers of such tales are usually too craven to make the slanderous charge that ministers are Communists, and they would have no evidence to go on if they did. But the accusers try in all sorts of devilish ways to tar with the Communist brush all ministers and Christian laymen who have a social concern and who apply their Christianity to the world in which they live.

It is true, of course, that there are such things as Communist front organizations and that they like nothing better than capturing respectable, Christian names as the façade behind which they pursue purposes which are neither respectable nor Christian. It is true that some ministers in their youthful naïveté or in their dotage join groups with respectable names and sign petitions wholly idealistic and humanitarian without investigating the people and the powers in the background. Later they discover that they have become the instrument, not of the Lord whom they are pledged to serve, but of men who have no respect for that Lord and no desire for his

Kingdom. The more complex our times become, the more impera-
tive it is that Christian ministers be "as wise as serpents."

The actual number of clergymen who have knowingly or inno-
cently joined Communist front organizations is small. The nation's
hatemongers have turned a few highly publicized cases into a massive condemnation of all ministers who have shown even a moder-
ate concern about social problems. Unfortunately this attack has
achieved a part of its purpose. It has intimidated some ministers.
Their fear of being called an ugly name has paralyzed all their
attempts to apply the gospel of Christ to the world he came to
save. The minister who qualifies today as an ambassador of Jesus
Christ must learn how to sail between these two dangers: the
danger of serving the wrong master and the danger of serving no
master at all.

The much talk about Communist front organizations deadens
our awareness of an equally dangerous, more widespread, and
much more subtle threat to Christian action in a needful world. I
refer to what we can call reactionary front organizations—groups
in the churches and outside which by title and purpose pretend to
promote Christian action but which actually prevent the kind of
Christian activity to which they appear to be devoted. In some
cities, for example, there are human relations councils which were
established for the ostensible and announced purpose of breaking
down racial barriers but which are dominated by racist members
who use the councils to soften and divert racial protests. Sometimes such councils are formed for the deliberate purpose of ab-
sorbing and dissipating Negroes' grievances before they come to a
head. Ministers who are deceived by such organizations may have
the best of intentions but by lending their names and influence to
such groups they actually subvert the worthy purposes which they
think they are serving.

Likewise, in some churches variously named committees of
Christian social concern serve as brakes on church action in dealing with controversial social problems. By devoting themselves
interminably to study and discussion such committees postpone
indefinitely the concrete action they were ostensibly established to
promote. In these churches social concerns committees are purely
ornamental; they give the churches an undeserved reputation for

social concern and by their existence develop among the people a complacency about the churches' duty to the world. In other churches the reactionary front organizations serve, like great sponges, to absorb and evaporate the devotion and resolution of those church members who want to thrust the church toward the world. Such churches get a name for one purpose but they serve another.

An impartial judge, standing apart from the church and the secular organization, would have to conclude that the uncommitted church—not secular society and not obstructionist cults—is not only the last bastion of racial segregation but also the ally of segregation. That this is not commonly understood is illustrated by a comment President Johnson made in the spring of 1964 when 6,000 Protestants, Catholics, and Jews met at Georgetown University in Washington to demand speedy passage of a strong civil rights bill. Mr. Johnson told 177 of their leaders, gathered in the East Room of the White House, that it was the mandate of America's religious community to "reawaken the conscience of your beloved land, the United States of America." If the priests, ministers, and rabbis attending this special White House conference were not momentarily dazzled by the President's flattery, they must have sensed in his remarks a touch either of mockery or of naïveté. In his characteristically ingratiating manner, and no doubt with the best of intentions, the President made assumptions which cannot survive close inspection.

First, the President implied that the racial problem in the United States lies outside the religious community and that the solution of the problem must come from within the religious community. The facts do not support this conclusion. The religious community in American society produced and sustained—sometimes on biblical grounds—the anti-Negro bias which has permeated the American mind from the beginning of the nation until the present day. Out of the nation's religious community came biblically and doctrinally supported theories of racial inferiority, and from this same source came immoral ethical codes which justified the exploitation of the Negro and demanded that the white man hold himself in sanctifying aloofness from the Negro.

Moreover—as I believe was proved unquestionably in my *The*

Racial Problem in Christian Perspective—the patterns of segregation which divide the common life of the country racially had their
beginning in the church before they found their perfection in the
secular society. It was not the secular world which infused the
church with contemptuous views of the Negro and imposed a segregated life on the Christian community. These offenses appeared
first in the religious community, even if we view the religious
community in its narrowest definition. The white man distorted the
Bible into a defense for slavery, and taught the Negro the passive
virtues of Christianity partly in the hope of making him tractable
and contented with his servile life. The white Christian in the
developing American culture confused Christianity with morality,
morality with gentility, and gentility with aloofness from the
Negro. As early as 1630, a bare 10 years after the arrival of the
first Negro slaves, white Christians condemned the crossing of the
racial line as an "abuse to the dishonor of God and shame of
Christians." Today, more than 300 years later, the air is full of
clichés which remind us that the religious community's old sin
against the Negro remains its current shame. Except for pioneering
leaders in some denominations and courageous ministers and laymen scattered here and there, the mass of white Christians is not
only confused and immobilized by the nation's racial crisis but is
also the major contributor to the nation's passivity.

If, in the President's words, it is the mandate of America's
religious community to reawaken the conscience of the land, who
will reawaken the conscience of the religious community? The
President's second false assumption identified the clergy as the
religious community and implied that the clergy can summon the
will and the energies of Christian people to a solution of the racial
problem.

We must distinguish between the clergy—a minority of which is
now committed to and active in the struggle for racial justice—and
the church, the religious community, the faithful—a still smaller
minority of which is committed to and active in the struggle for
racial justice. Both of these minorities working together have not
been able thus far to swing the great bulk of religious America into
the crusade for an integrated America free of racial discrimination.

Within a month after President Johnson pleaded with the ministers, priests, rabbis, and leading church laymen in the White House, Alabama's Governor Wallace received 43 percent of the Democratic Presidential primary vote in Maryland. Louisiana's segregationist Senator Allen J. Ellender noted in a speech before the Senate that the Maryland clergy—he exaggerated the number—failed to reduce support for Wallace: "All the preachers, all the rabbis, all the priests in Maryland—and there are many of them," he said, "were preaching 'Vote for Brewster and against Wallace, the racist, the segregationist.' "

Georgia's Senator Richard Russell derided the clergy's influence in Maryland. "In the course of his campaign Governor Wallace was picketed and lampooned at almost every appearance he made," Senator Russell said. "Men of the cloth picketed his meetings carrying highly critical signs."

An Associated Press summary of the Maryland campaign provided the sobering fact which enabled the southern Senators to dismiss the clergy as an influential factor in the campaign: "Wallace polled most heavily among Catholics, who comprise a large percentage of both the Baltimore city and Baltimore suburban votes. Substantially more than half of the state's Catholic voters cast their ballots for Wallace. . . . Wallace edged Brewster among white Anglo-Saxon Protestants."

The Maryland campaign demonstrated what politicians have long held to be an axiomatic fact of American politics: On most social issues—whatever the religious overtones of those issues—the clergy cannot deliver the votes of its people. The clergy is particularly inept when there are members of it on both sides of the issue. The religious community exuberantly sings of itself in the gospel song: "Like a mighty army moves the church of God." But this view of the church ignores that army's refusal to occupy the beachheads of racial justice secured for it at great personal sacrifice by some members of the clerical corps. As someone has put it, white clergymen who daringly champion the Negro in the racial struggle are generals without an army.

Informed Protestants have long known that Protestant ministers can speak officially for their people only when they declare conventional truths, echo the prejudices of their people, or comment on pious, other-worldly matters. They have assumed that, though

Protestant clergymen cannot deliver the votes of their people on social and political issues, Roman Catholic clergymen can.

The Alabama Governor proved in Maryland and Wisconsin— specifically in Baltimore and Milwaukee—that for many Roman Catholics the racial issue transcends loyalty to the priest. In both states diocesan papers as well as local priests threw the weight of the church against Governor Wallace. Yet Roman Catholics in both areas, translating the racial problem into terms of residence and job security, defied the clergy and voted for the segregationist. This is not to say that the influence of priests and pastors over their parishioners is completely defunct. What it does say is that in areas of racial tension the influence of clergymen has to be exemplary rather than commanding, educational rather than directive, inspirational rather than mandatory. In the racial struggle as nowhere else we find depressing evidence that the long-time diminishing influence of the clergy over the people now reaches its nadir. Granted that most clergymen still have the loyalty, affection, and gratitude of the people they serve, these affections are not enough to make most laymen follow their clergymen into the social arenas. Nor should it be forgotten that there are many laymen who are personally offended when their ministers enter controversial areas they will not enter themselves.

In every church there is a nub of laymen who believe the minister is a hireling, a paid guest speaker, whose business it is not to declare from the pulpit the often offensive judgments and sometimes humiliating mercies of God but to echo instead the mind and the mood of the people. Not infrequently these laymen are sufficiently powerful to execute their threat to remove the minister from his charge if his words from the pulpit or his deeds in the social order challenge the people's racial practices. Indeed, in Protestant churches the transferring of ministers who speak and act for racial justice to other parishes or the outright firing of such ministers occurs with increasing frequency.

But the whole blame for the detachment of most of the church from the struggle for racial justice must not be put on the laity. Time and again the minister who has been challenged to step out of his ministerial anonymity and the security of silence and inactivity and champion some radical but plainly Christian position in the racial struggle offers the excuse, "I must maintain communication with my people."

For some ministers this pat answer is an escape, a refuge, a dodge. There is a modicum of truth in it and they can rely upon that truth to conceal the true motivation of their withdrawal from the struggle. For some ministers this answer is a protection against immoderate words or unconventional acts which would jeopardize their sinecures. For some the answer rises out of fear. It isn't easy: a wife to support, two children ready for college, a cantankerous bishop to please, the payments on the car, a building fund newly launched—these things can make cowards of us all.

But who are a clergyman's "people"? The few whom he has a contract to serve or the many whom he has a covenant to serve? Are not the poor, the broken-hearted, the captives, the blind, the bruised, the oppressed, the ostracized, every clergyman's "people" whether or not they are members of his parish?

Here and there the church stirs as though it may yet wake to its duty to oppressed, excluded, exploited Negro America. Young ministers are breaking the fetters with which the institutional church binds them. Roman Catholic priests recently condemned their archbishop in California for his dilatory approach to the racial problem. And subsequently one of these priests fled from the repressive air which saturates Cardinal McIntyre's Los Angeles Archdiocese to the less restrictive presence of Chicago's now deceased Cardinal Meyer. Older clergymen in all faiths now and then take their church's solutions seriously and sometimes for their daring find themselves in jail. Small groups of committed laymen are trying here and there to live out in the hazardous act and the courageous word the ethical meanings of their faith.

But for most American Christians the local church remains the last innermost fortress defending their segregated personal lives from the presence of the Negro. Racial segregation is purposefully built into the site, structure, and spirit of these churches. Racial segregation is one of their chief reasons for being.

Some time back I preached at the dedication of a new church building in Deerfield, Illinois. Remembering that the village fathers in Deerfield had circumvented the moving of Negroes into that all-white town by condemning and buying the sites on which Negroes had planned to build, I felt compelled to tell these racially secluded Christians that until white Protestantism, flinging its doors open to people, ceases being exclusively white it cannot escape the socio-logical trap in which it now strangles, that God will pass by the Gothic mausoleums, the modernistic sepulchers, in which white Protestantism lies splendidly attired for burial, and in a strange new way will build *his* new church. Afterward one of the laymen said, "We agree with everything you say, but why tell us? We have no Negroes in our town." How do you explain to that kind of mentality that *it* is the problem? How do you explain to such Christians—otherwise fine people—that the Negro problem is in-significant, that the *Negro's* problem is immense, and that every village and town which arbitrarily shuts him out is itself one of the nation's toughest, ugliest, and most destructive problems? How can you persuade people to let Negroes move into their villages when they were driven to the suburbs by their racial prejudices? How do you involve suburban churches in the struggle for racial justice when their reason for being is in part racial? Who will reawaken the consciences of such religious communities?

It can no longer be claimed that the church does not know the error of its ways, that it does not by its own codes know what is right and what it should do. President Kennedy and after him President Johnson labeled the struggle for the abolishment of all racial discrimination an economic, social, political, international, and, most of all, moral issue. This declaration by the President of the United States and an earlier, similar one by his predecessor place the racial problem in proper context. At last the ethical implications of the nation's political and religious creeds—so long obscured and ignored—receive formal, unequivocal, open en-dorsement at the highest level of government.

Few white Americans, few white Christians, will take exception to their President's definition of the racial problem as a moral issue. The day has passed when intelligent, informed, honest people can salve their consciences by using theological and biblical justifications for the segregation and exploitation of the Negro. The exclusion and the oppression of Negroes continue as ugly patterns in American society; but the souls of many white people, convinced that the patterns are ugly, are ashamed of them even when they do nothing to change the lot of American Negroes. Before they could appeal to the churches to placate their consciences; now every major religious body in the United States—at least in its official edicts and resolutions—condemns racial segregation and discrimination as wrong, immoral, an offense to God as well as to fellowman.

Although this mood of shame, guilt, and deep unrest is not universal, it is sufficiently widespread to be termed a prevailing white American attitude toward the racial problem in the sixth decade of the twentieth century. And this mood, like the old one it has gradually displaced, needs careful diagnosis. Certainly it is much more wholesome than that ambivalent American mind which in the eighteenth century wrote glowing descriptions of human freedom and equality with one pen and slave codes with another. The present American temper is more honest and creative than that of the nineteenth century which half-heartedly freed the slave and then whole-heartedly ostracized him from the mainstreams of American life.

Even so this current American mood—the white man's feelings of guilt and shame over his racial conduct and his failure to translate his feeling of racial immorality into creative action—imperils the white man's soul and the Negro's whole life. The Negro today is more amused than cajoled by the white man's breast-beating. He weighs the white man's confessions of racial guilt against society's failure to put professed ideals into concrete deeds and finds something wanting. And what he finds wanting is what interests him most—not redeemed white attitudes and profuse white apologies but job equality, integrated neighborhoods, desegrated public facilities. Some Negroes may be concerned about the state of the white man's soul and may rejoice that the white man's conscience now senses remorsefully the evil of his racial deeds. Most Negroes, however, are not impressed by a repentant mood which produces no reform of the white man's racial conduct.

Neither is this mood good for the white man. To keep on doing what one knows to be grossly evil or to hold ideals which one never tries to put into practice are psychologically dangerous exercises. Inevitably they end in callousness or in morbidity. If the white man, knowing now that he sins against the Negro and suffering

now the guilt of that sin, fails to take the next step—the step which
leads to just and charitable deeds, to practical actions which open
to Negroes an equitable share in the blessings and burdens of
American society, to desegregated communities, to equalized educational and employment opportunities and wide-open public facilities—his sense of guilt will turn into a neurotic public exhibition
which compounds his sin against himself and against the Negro. In
the racial struggle the time for confession, moralizing, and the
sentimental preaching of vague generalities has passed. To go further in this direction is futile and perilous. A line from a popular
song runs, "What can I say, dear, after I've said I'm sorry?" The
answer is that you cannot *say* anything. You must then *do* something. If white people sincerely believe that the racial struggle is a
moral issue, if they are in earnest in confessing their sins against
the Negro, why do they not "bring forth therefore fruits worthy of
repentance." Let us now turn to some answers to this question.

4

Understanding the Present Dilemma

One of the Swiss coats of arms carries a slogan which summarizes the biblical view of all human experience. It reads: "History is governed by human confusion and by divine providence." The first part of this slogan gives us no trouble intellectually. We have seen in the white man's old and continuing ambivalence toward the Negro and his vacillation in dealing with the Negro abundant confirmations of the fact that interracial history is governed by human confusion. Long before we had any responsibility for it the racial problem in this country was created and perpetuated by human confusion rising from conflicting greed and generosity, pride and humbleness, cravenness and courage, concern and indifference. And long after the present generation of Christians could have resolved some of this confusion, it still remains. Why? Must we blame our bewilderment and our inactivity in the face of racial oppression entirely on vicious racial hatred or are there less damning but equally embarrassing explanations? Granted that racial prejudice is the principal answer to the question "Why doesn't the church do something about the racial problem?" But there are also reasons why our racial goodwill, such as we have, takes no concrete form. Let us examine some of the sources of our ethical confusion.

First, Christians are stunned and stymied by the racial problem's sheer massiveness. Even its geographic immensity compounds our inherited quandary. The proportion of Negroes to whites in the American population has steadily dropped from a high of 19.3 percent in 1790 to 10.5 percent in 1960. Several factors produced a declining proportion of Negroes: a continuous and sometimes heavy immigration of white Europeans to the United States, a higher mortality rate among Negroes than among whites, and the passing of many light-skinned people from the category of Negroes to that of whites. But the spread of Negroes from the deep South into the North and West and the hostilities which met them give the racial conflict a geographic scope which it did not have 50 years ago. The datelines on the stories of Negro-white clashes move north; Birmingham, Jackson, St. Augustine, are matched by Cleveland, Brooklyn, Chicago. From one coast to the other, north and south, the whole nation is involved. If guilt demands the company misery loves, white southerners have plenty of company in racial guilt.

The problem is confusingly massive not only in its geographic spread but also in its penetration of the whole fabric of American life. The issue cannot be isolated and quarantined as though it were exclusively economic or educational, personal or political. It flows into every stratum of the psychic and social orders. Being as it is *the* problem in the nation's soul, it radiates into every area of the nation's life. From the physical and spiritual deprivation of the littlest child in a Negro ghetto to the nation's loss of international prestige this problem dyes the whole cloth of our country's life. You cannot pick up any American problem without taking up the racial problem with it. Some years ago a white woman in a northern city, replying to my wife's telephone plea for help on an interracial committee, said, "I'm sorry, Mrs. Haselden, but I've dropped human relations for this year." Perhaps this was more a slip of the tongue than a lapse of concern. It takes a spiritual contortionist to wrench himself free of the racial problem and he has to drop all human relations to do it. Health, the handicapped, education, employment, the church, politics—if you make any one of these your Christian concern, you will find that the racial conflict clings to and penetrates that concern. The racial problem in American society is therefore not *a* problem; it is an epidemic disease which infects and weakens and mortally endangers every cell of the personal and civil body. Massive in its geographic scope, the racial problem is equally massive in its penetration of the people's total life.

Second, Christians are confused and immobilized by the speed with which the racial problem unfolds and frantically seeks its solution in this generation. No Negro faithful to his people's hopes and no white man who shares those hopes will accept the racial progress of the past score of years as an argument for gradualism or as an excuse for the white man's inactivity. But it remains true that the Negro quest for justice, so long getting off the pad, now soars like a rocket. The speed with which racial barriers fell in the secular world during the past 20 years astounds anyone whose adult experience covered the 1920's and 30's. As I write this in 1965 I hear Edwin C. Berry, executive secretary of the Chicago Urban League say over radio: "Last year I said that we were 50 percent of the way toward democracy in Chicago; this year I say we are 60 percent on the way. Sixty percent is a long way from 100 percent, but a ten percent gain in one year is remarkable." Indeed so, and there are signs that the rate of racial progress will accelerate even more astoundingly in the years ahead in all fields except the churches and the social clubs.

However, white Christians are not so much baffled and certainly not so much immobilized by the progress of race relations as they are by the forms of Negro protest which have secured that progress. The Negro's struggle against oppressive white rule began a long time before Martin Luther King, Jr., was born. The techniques which he employed—non-violent non-cooperation—are as old as Judeo-Christian history. In this country Henry David Thoreau defined and practiced the principles of his *Civil Disobedience* more than a hundred years ago. Labor unions have used non-cooperation in the form of strikes most effectively. Even so, when Mrs. Rosa Parks, a Montgomery, Alabama, Negro seamstress, refused on December 5, 1955, to follow custom and sit in the rear of a public bus, King, a student of Gandhi's methods in India, organized around that incident the now famous Montgomery bus boycott and initiated a wave of non-violent protests against racial injustice. Though this kind of struggle had been tried by Negroes before and had failed, now its moment has come. "The time appeared to be ripe for a nearly universal response by the Negro community; federal law was favorable, and there was widespread concern about what 'image' the United States would have abroad were segregation to continue. Moreover, the economic position of the Negro, bad as it continued to be, was improving. A new sense of self-confidence, too, was abroad among members of the younger generation, many of them now attending college; and fresh leadership within the ranks of Negro ministers—witness the career of the Reverend Dr. Martin Luther King, Jr.—initiated an often deep religious commitment to non-violence."[1]

The words in which Nehru described Gandhi's non-violent weapon—*satyagraha*—can be applied almost verbatim to the Negro's non-violent protest: " . . . this voice was somehow different from the others. It was quiet and low, and yet it could be heard above the shouting of the multitude; it was soft and gentle, and yet there seemed to be steel hidden away somewhere in it; it was courteous and full of appeal, and yet there was something grim and frightening in it; every word used was full of meaning and seemed to carry a deadly earnestness. Behind the language of peace and friendship there was power and the quivering shadow of action and a determination not to submit to a wrong."[2] The non-violent yet coercive and effective weapon which Gandhi used against the repressive Rowlatt acts in India in 1919, King and his followers drew in 1955 against repressive racial laws and customs. Their method was not pacifism but a new kind of racial warfare, a warfare which renounced hostility—either physical or verbal—against human beings but which exerted tremendous real and suggested pressure. That year marked the end of the Negro's humble, grovelling, passive non-resistance broken by occasional physical outbursts. The new day had come—the day of dedicated, disciplined non-violent warfare against the oppressors and their oppressive systems.

In the months following this Montgomery, Alabama, event there erupted over the South and in some parts of the North so many sit-ins, wade-ins, kneel-ins, and freedom rides that the racists saw in this fact a conspiracy, a highly organized Communist plot. They could not believe that the Negro himself was capable of devising, engineering, and courageously conducting such a daring and effec-

1. From THE QUIET BATTLE edited by Mulford Q. Sibley, copyright © 1963 by Mulford Q. Sibley. Reprinted by permission of Doubleday & Company, Inc. P. 289.
2. Copyright © 1942 by The John Day Company, Inc. Reprinted from GLIMPSES OF WORLD HISTORY by Jawaharlal Nehru by permission of The John Day Company, Inc., publisher. P. 713.

tive rebellion against unjust laws and stifling customs. The racists were wrong. Knowing full well what they were doing, Negroes in scattered parts of the country broke local laws and violated local customs which bemeaned their dignity and deprived them of their rights and of the benefits guaranteed to them not only by the federal government but also by moral law. They courted unjust imprisonment as a means of pricking the conscience of the nation and laying claim to their rights as full citizens. And they went to jail gladly, rejoicing in the fact that in some cases they overflowed the jails and compelled the white man to build stockades to hold them.

In all of this the Negro knew and the white man was appalled to discover that though the Negro's warfare was "soft and gentle" there was "steel hidden away somewhere in it." The Negro could afford to use "the language of peace and friendship" because he sensed and he knew that the white man would sense that behind this language there was "power and the quivering shadow of action." And though the Negro's protest was "courteous and full of appeal"—perhaps for this reason—it was "grim and frightening." For one thing, the novel form which the Negro's struggle took in those years compelled racists to take a new look at the Negro and what they saw baffled them. The racists discovered that they had been betrayed by their own cherished clichés. This man challenging white supremacy, white laws, white traditions, was no cowardly, grovelling dullard. On the contrary, here standing defiantly over against the white man were proud, intelligent Negroes, determined and contemptuous of the consequences. What do you do with men and women who endure beatings, welcome imprisonment, and appear willing to die for their cause? A new view of the Negro was thrust upon the racist and, since the racist's self-consciousness rested in large part upon his stereotyping of the Negro, this new type of racial protest jarred and shattered the racist's image of himself. For many white people this was indeed a grim and frightening business. Where race prejudice is the knot in which all the strands of personality are tied together, the severing or the threatened severing of that knot can cause psychological disasters. This disaster happens to many white people whose personalities are held together by their cherished myths about the Negro. The Negro who appears in the new form of racial protest steals from the white man the comforting stereotypes to which he has become addicted.

Again, the non-violent, non-cooperative forms of racial struggle were frightening to the so-called "moderates" in race relations, to those Christians who have been willing to champion the Negro's cause verbally and in personal acts of charity but who have been unwilling to participate personally in a radical restructuring of social patterns. In his push toward justice the Negro put to the moderates a challenge which can best be conveyed in the language of the gambler: "Put up or shut up!" But "putting up"—as we shall note toward the end of this chapter—requires action and the one thing most Christians do not want to be involved in is action. Moreover, to many Christian moderates—including some Negroes —sit-ins, boycotts, and freedom rides seemed a bit uncouth, un-dignified. (A few years ago I was talking on a college campus with a Negro leader who must be included in any list of the ten people who have done the most for Negroes in this century. Negroes owe him too much and I have too much respect for him to reveal his name. In substance this Negro leader said: "I look on in stunned admiration at what these young Negroes and whites are doing to secure justice for Negroes; but going to jail voluntarily . . . I'm afraid I couldn't do it.") There are many conscientious Christians, white and Negro, who share his reservations. Their self-respect requires gentility, orderliness, due process, good manners. So long as they could help the Negro and at the same time keep these dimensions of their personality, they were willing to do so. But the new racial struggle requires that they enlist on its terms, not theirs. It leaves—perhaps unfortunately—little ground for the moderates to stand on.

Furthermore, the Negro's new drive for his place in the main-stream of American life became a grim and frightening business for the nation. The naïve and the pompous say that it does not matter what the rest of the world thinks about the United States, but refutations of this boast come everyday from every part of the world. The shame and the weakness of the nation was exposed when the world saw that the Negro had to launch a non-violent revolution to claim what the laws of the country guarantee to all its citizens. The enemies of the United States do not need to fabricate scurrilous propaganda in order to discredit the intentions of the United States in its dealings with the colored peoples of the world. They need only to report in the Congo, in Laos, in Vietnam, in Venezuela, what has actually happened in Alabama, Mississippi, Chicago, and Philadelphia. The most devastating propaganda circulated against the United States from Moscow and Peking is written in the deeds done in the Deep South and in the racial ghettos of northern cities. The new racial protest exposed and dramatized the nation's offenses against the Negro, and made news of worldwide interest out of the traditional, commonplace abuses suffered by nations. And this was a principal factor in the passage of the Civil Rights Bill in 1964.

The Negro's coercive, non-violent forms of protest are grim business for white churches when the Negro attempts to crash the color barrier in the churches. Whether such attempts succeed or fail, they publicize the churches' failure to practice at home what they preach abroad. Missionaries can no longer cover up the embarrassing fact that while they are trying to win converts among colored people abroad their churches exclude colored people at home. Nor are colored peoples abroad willing to accept any longer the missionaries' explanation that racial exclusiveness in the churches is the product of a few extremists. To be sure, what deadens and thwarts the missionary movement in various parts of the world is the white churches' sinful exclusion of Negroes and not the Negroes' exposure of that evil by attempts to enter racially exclusive churches. But the push toward an integrated church compels the churches either to accept Negroes and lose some racist white members or to reject Negroes and deal foreign missions a blow from which it cannot recover.

A case in point occurred at the First Baptist Church of Richmond, Virginia, in January 1965. Two Nigerian students at Virginia Union University in Richmond—Adedokun Oshoniyi and Bisi Adegbile—kept a New Year's resolution and presented themselves for membership in the all-white First Baptist Church. They did so on their own initiative but also under pressure from their fathers, both Baptist ministers in Nigeria and converts of Southern Baptist missions in that country. The Richmond First Baptist Church does not exclude Negroes from its worship services but since 1840 it has excluded Negroes from its membership. Its minister, Theodore F. Adams, a former president of the Baptist World Alliance, is widely respected as a clergyman and has been honored by the National Conference of Christians and Jews for "life-time devotion to the idea of the brotherhood of man under the Fatherhood of God." When the Nigerian students applied for church membership, Dr. Adams urged his board of deacons to open the membership to anyone "acknowledging Jesus Christ as his savior and lord." The board turned down the applications by a narrow margin. The following Sunday in his morning sermon Dr. Adams appealed to his congregation to grasp the pressing problem facing the church "in the spirit of Christian love, without other consideration." The deacons then met again and prepared three recommendations for the 4,200 members of the church to consider: (1) to accept the Nigerians as student members, (2) to study the church's admission policy "in the light of changed world conditions," (3) to admit no other Negro members until the study had been completed. After four hours of deliberation by 1,800 of the church's members, the church voted to admit the Nigerian students into full church membership, thus reversing the deacons' decision, and to accept the second and third recommendations of the board.

It could be that this short step toward an integrated church in the South was accomplished "without other consideration." It is more likely that the location of the church building less than a mile from the headquarters building of the Southern Baptist Convention's Foreign Missions Board had some influence upon the decision to admit Nigerians. Certainly the missionary significance of the decision was not missed by the Nigerian sons of Baptist pastors. In reporting the incident to *The Christian Century*, correspondent Sue Nichols quoted Adegbile as saying: "This vote is going to have a great impact on missions. Ever since this thing started, all eyes at home have been on it. Now that the decision is positive, people at home will be happy. Missionaries will be able to tell Nigerians that people here try to practice Christianity as they preach it."

For still another reason the Negro's new form of rebellion is frightening for whites and grim business for Negro leaders. Behind non-violent action lies the possibility of violent action. The bloodless rebellion can if mishandled become a bloody one. On three occasions between 1919 and 1922 Gandhi's followers, inadequately disciplined in the techniques of *satyagraha,* resorted to mob violence. On each occasion Gandhi called off his crusade, over the objections of his closest associates, and did personal penance through fasting for the damage his people, run amuck, had done to other people and to property. The same peril with the same disastrous possibilities faces the peaceful rebellion of American Negroes. If non-violence, non-cooperation, and the breaking of unjust local laws—legitimate forms of Negro protest— degenerate into mob violence or even into a vengeful harassment of the white man unrelated to a specific oppression, the Negro's progress will suffer a tragic reversal. It will lose not only its moral justification but also its effectiveness. White racists know how to deal with and to overcome violent forms of force; they do not know how to cope with non-violent power. When a physically powerful Negro woman in Selma, Alabama, stepped out of the picket line and struck the sheriff, she betrayed King's movement in two ways: she deserted the non-violent disciplines she had been taught and she gave the sheriff and his deputies an excuse for using the only kind of power they know how to use.

But the danger is not so much that men like Martin Luther King, Jr., and movements like his will turn to senseless rioting as it is that such leaders and movements will be displaced by others which either spurn non-violence or use it as a temporary device. There are Negro leaders who believe that the time has come for Negroes to unleash their brute power in the struggle for justice. Such a course of action will be met by an equally ruthless and physically superior white power, will destroy the gains the Negro has already achieved, and will postpone indefinitely the integration which should follow the desegregation of the races. Moreover, this kind of protest stiffens white resistance and produces—as in the fall of 1964—a white backlash.

White Christians who withdraw from all forms of social action which champion the Negro's cause because they fear what might happen; whose too lively imaginations see the worst that can be rather than the generally well-disciplined, restrained protest that is; who view every orderly demonstration as a potential race riot; who fear that the breaking of unjust laws is automatically a threat to just laws—such Christians undercut responsible Negro leaders and by delaying the coming of racial justice strengthen the hands of irresponsible Negro racists. Only by helping King's kind of protest succeed can white Christians prevent the racial violence which they fear. The fears which immobilize white Christians are irrational. In a fine sense, they are not fears at all but anxieties. That is, the alarm is disproportionate to the danger. Nevertheless, we have to concede as a statement of fact that the speed and novelty of present-day Negro protest against injustice paralyze many white Christian moderates.

A few years ago James T. McCain, a South Carolina field secretary for the Congress of Racial Equality, declared: "The Emancipation Proclamation freed the Negro physically; the Supreme Court freed him mentally." Since that time the Congress of the United States in the 1964 Civil Rights Bill in an increased measure freed the Negro socially. In a small degree the white Christian church has participated in each of these liberations. What the white Christian church now needs to do is to free *itself* spiritually. The greater numbers of its people are stunned, provoked, and alarmed by what the Negro is doing to free himself from the shackles that remain and by their fearful uncertainty about what the Negro will do next. White Christians cannot escape from this mental and emotional prison so long as they think of the racial struggle in terms of "we" and "they." What many white Christians fear most—the coming of Negroes into their churches—is what they most need if their anxieties are to be resolved. And what many Christians dread most—involvement in the racial struggle— they will find less dreadful when in spiritual identity with the Negro they get on the right side of the struggle.

Third, Christians are confused and inactive because it is difficult for the problem to understand the problem. Direct participation by the church in active solutions of the racial problems requires a confession of guilt, for the church continues to be the problem. The character and course of the racial struggle in the United States —whether creative or calamitous—do not depend primarily on Negro leaders and their zealous white allies but on the extent to which the great mainstream of white Christian America turns over the racial struggle to rabid, racial extremists on both sides of the racial struggle. Suddenly—as put editorially in *The Christian Century*—the white man discovers that two Samsons grasp with powerfully destructive arms at the supporting pillars of the nation's house, both wantonly determined to have their will in their own way or pull the house down upon themselves and everyone else. Too long responsible white people turned over the Negro to one of these giants—the entrenched leadership of uncompromising racial segregation and discrimination. This threatening giant is blind in both eyes: His cause is evil and his method is mad. Determined to keep the Negro a suppressed and exploitable menial, needing a humiliated Negro to inflate his own self-respect, the white racist unconditionally opposes any social, legislative, or religious recognition of the Negro as a man, a citizen, or a brother. This blind, bungling segregationist giant applies the crudest of all instruments to the most complex and delicate and social problem confronting the nation. The only weapons he knows are guns, fire hoses, cattle prodders, police dogs, bombs, night sticks, and filthy jails. So he is not only immoral and brutal; he is also stupid. Against an aroused, self-confident Negro who has righteousness on his side, white comrades in his ranks, and the United States Constitution at his back, terroristic methods will no longer work. Such weapons can create havoc and bloody heads, break hearts, and incite Negroes to similar tactics, but they will not prevent the continuing desegregation of America's public life.

The second giant groping his way toward the pillars of the house has good sight in one eye but is blind in the other: His end is righteous but his means are deranged. Blame the recalcitrant white racists for the imbecility of the methods adopted by some Negroes and some whites at the extreme wings of racial protest, and you are close to the truth. It should not be surprising that desperate and despairing Negroes and their white supporters should now and then strike out in spasms of violence and irrational passion. Be surprised rather by the Negro's phenomenal patience, his disciplined restraint, his consistent appeal to the nation's code and creed and to the white man's conscience. But bad judgment, however explained and justified, remains bad judgment and remains disastrous. The outraged and enraged Negro has no option. He must protest, must struggle for his full place in the nation's life, must use every commandable, controllable instrument to secure for himself and his children the heritage of free men. But if he follows those leaders, white or Negro, who make recklessness the test of loyalty and the rightness of their goal the sanction of any means to attain that goal, the Negro commits suicide, pulling the house down on himself.

But there is a more important question which touches the heart of the matter. Who is responsible for the fact that leadership in the racial struggle swings toward the fanatical extremes of that struggle? Who surrenders racial justice to immorality and bad judgment? Who creates the vacuum for white extremists and Negro extremists? The sober and precise answer to these questions points an indicting finger at the unmoved, indifferent white-created and white-controlled power structures in American society: churches, governments, professional and social fraternities, and the intricate networks of finance, commerce, and management. The indicting finger which probes the constituency of obstructionist social structures finds cultured, genteel, gentle people—predominantly Christian people—who would recoil in righteous shock from any hint that they are responsible for the rigid systems which bind the Negro in humiliating inequities and which torment him into irrational outbursts. Nevertheless, not the extremists but the power structures which embrace and serve mainstream America produce and preserve the racial chasm in American society. If those structures remain indifferent, inflexible, inactive, before the Negro's plight and protest, the blind and half-blind giants, ruthless and reckless, will imperil the whole house.

Fourth, white Christians withdraw from the racial struggle in confusion because they fail to credit to Negroes the same kind of emotional reactions that they experience themselves. When the Negro's protest against racial injustice veers under reckless leadership from non-violence to harrassment to violence, white people should remember the hard, principal fact that the Negro's grievance is real, old, deep, and unbearable. When the protest takes on aberrant forms, when to the white mind it appears wholly irresponsible and entirely vengeful, this is no time for white people to lose patience with Negroes whose patience has run out. If some

Negroes and some of their white supporters adopt tactics which some white Christians cannot approve, if they confuse obstruction with action and turn non-violence into reckless forms of violence, white Christians should not let such actions blind them to their guilt and their people's shame. Many white people and some Negroes wholly committed to a total acceptance of the Negro in all areas of American life are nevertheless withheld from merely vengeful or harassing tactics by their good judgment and by ethical disciplines which will not permit them to engage in the extremists' guerrilla warfare. But such whites and Negroes discredit their denunciation of extremists if they refuse to perform in the areas of racial conflict those deeds which wisdom and morality permit and which the urgencies of the conflict demand.

Even more tragic and unjust is that impatience with all Negroes which rises in white moderates when the fringes of the Negro protest turn to violence. The recklessness of a few extremists in Brooklyn does not exorcise the guilt of white America or alter in the slightest the cruel affliction white America has long imposed on Negro America. When I was a boy in the South I heard in our rural setting that some animals caught in steel traps will gnaw off their legs to escape. The fact that they are maimed for life or bleed to death may say something about them but it says nothing about the trap. Man, white or Negro, is that kind of animal. Under provocation he will go to self-mutilating extremes to escape from the trap. The Negro is caught in a vicious trap which the white man set. Responsible white people will not abandon all Negroes because some mutilate themselves and harm their cause in violent efforts to escape. Frenzied action by desperate Negroes increases the need for Christian patience and Christian action.

Fifth, white Christians are confused and immobilized because the Negro will not settle for the much he has gained but insists that he must as a man and a citizen have all that belongs to a man and a citizen, must have it now, and must have it here. In *Change in the Contemporary South* Edgar T. Thompson put the explanation categorically and what he said will appear to thoughtful men as axiomatic: "The narrower the status gap becomes the more sensitive are men to the differences that remain. The gains American Negroes have recently made can be expected to promote more, not less, dissatisfaction on their part."[3] We can extend this thought logically and psychologically: The narrower the gap the more rigorously will Negroes struggle to close the gap altogether.

Negroes are fully aware of the fact that though their pilgrimage to full freedom has been tormentingly slow, they have nevertheless made progress. It does not look as big to them as it does to the white man, but they know that they fare better in a white-dominated society than did their fathers. Why does this knowledge inflame Negroes to a more rigorous protest than their fathers made against slavery? Why, reasons the white man in his bafflement, do they claim so much more when comparatively they have gained so much? The answer is elemental. In his maturity man is not satisfied with *some* when he knows the value of *all.* As he reaches the fullness of his maturity he senses the humiliating disparity between *some* and *all,* between the fragment of his rights which he does have and the parcel of his rights which he does not have.

While many Negroes in slavery yearned only for freedom, some Negroes like Frederick Douglass yearned for freedom plus. Everything the white man claimed as man and citizen, sensitive, alert Douglass claimed for himself. Time and circumstance have in our day multiplied Frederick Douglass 10,000 times. While some Negroes after slavery found it necessary to hide their resentment from white people, bite their tongues, and get along the best way they could, W. E. B. Du Bois—brilliant, fiery, courageous—was letting white people know in no uncertain terms what he thought of their contemptible racial hypocrisies. Time and circumstance have multiplied W. E. B. Du Bois 10,000 times. While some Negroes were still bowing and scraping and doffing their caps before white people, the Howard University sociologist Kelly Miller was puncturing the white man's pride with a rapier-like pen. Time and circumstance have multiplied Kelly Miller 10,000 times. There is no such thing as "the new Negro," if it means a new species or brand of Negro. The United States had 75 years ago every kind of protest it has today, but time and circumstance have permitted the real Negro to emerge in multiplied duplicates of Douglass, Du Bois, Miller. These three who, being men, would not be content with

---

3. *Change in the Contemporary South, op. cit.,* p. 104.

anything less than their full right as men, have in our day innumerable heirs who despise the diminishing gap between *some* and *all* even more than their fathers did the huge gap between *nothing* and *some*. As the gap closes and the Negro's resentment increases, white Christians should see in this development not petulance or spite on the part of the Negro but the emergence of a people into full awareness of their rights and their dignities.

Sixth, white Christians are confused and immobilized by their misunderstanding of the nature of conflict and the role of conflict in the solution of social problems. Since action invariably uncovers conflict, they conclude that they must not act. The ironic fact is that while confession of racial guilt by individual Christians becomes relatively easy, indeed almost popular with some Christians in our day, action remains difficult. It is always easier to preach than to practice, to repent than to reform. As the Danish theologian Kierkegaard saw clearly, the most daring idealistic words are permitted provided one does not put them into action. In his *Journals* Kierkegaard wrote words which are now the most accurate explanation of Christian inactivity in the field of racial struggle: "The moment I take Christianity as a doctrine and so indulge my cleverness or profundity or my eloquence or my imaginative powers in depicting it, people are very pleased; I am looked upon as a serious Christian. The moment I begin to express existentially what I say, and consequently to bring Christianity into reality, it is just as though I had exploded existence—the scandal is there at once."

Kierkegaard believed that the lone individual must daringly make the leap from speculation to action but that when he does so he must expect decision and action to explode existence—his personal existence and the environment in which he exists. In his view the Christian must neither retreat into himself nor lose himself in the crowd. He must be an individual and as an individual he must act. But he must know as he does so that action drops depth charges into the pit of his being, exploding him and his society.

This, then, is the dilemma faced by many white people when they approach the racial struggle. They know what they should do, what indeed they want to do. But they sense also the peril of action. They know that action explodes their personal, individual existence. If they meet Negroes on the level of unfeigned equality, champion the rights of Negroes to enter forbidden areas of society, join a march or a picket line, sell their house to a Negro buyer, or in a thousand less dramatic ways live with Negroes as they do with white people, they substitute one set of tensions for another. For the act of racial goodwill is a commitment. It puts one on record with oneself in an irrefutable way. It pins one down, limits the range of options for future actions. Once he acts a man is no longer what he was. The affirmative deed rebukes and challenges what he was, raising a conflict between his old self and his new. The act must defend itself against lingering doubts and reservations. Questions arise: Was I a fool? Did I go too far? Were my motivations genuine or spurious? Did I permit myself to be pushed over the edge of decision solely because I wanted to be popular with those who expect this sort of thing? Was I stampeded by one crowd to take steps I will regret when I am with another crowd? Did I do more harm than good? How will I explain this unusual behavior to friends and loved ones who do not share my racial views? Such questions gradually disappear as the solitary acts of goodwill become a pattern of life, but they can be tormenting for the soul when it makes its first ventures across the line between profession and deed.

Moreover, the initial act of racial goodwill explodes the individual's personal existence by hurling his contradictory ideals and ideas against one another. None of us has a simple inheritance of consistent and complementary attitudes. All of us absorb from parents and society a motley accumulation of mental and emotional dispositions. Willy-nilly we take into our systems some of the prejudices and superstitions as well as some of the aspiration and wisdom of the race. The deed activates these latent antagonisms, musters them into opposite camps, and draws for them a line of battle. The act makes it impossible for conflicting racial ideas to remain at peace with one another. For the sensitive novice in the field of racial action the soul becomes a battlefield for the struggle of manners and morals, prudence and daring, taste and resolution, reticence and boldness. In him the desire for acceptance tempts his obedience to his convictions; his hunger for life's placid simplicities resists the demands of life's buffeting moral dilemmas; and his identity with and loyalty to family and class and friends conflict with his loyalty to his new view of his moral duty. It is not easy to act and to act responsibly in ways contrary to early training, to deeply embedded prejudices, to innate self-centeredness, and to the mores of one's social group. Action generates unwelcomed tension; action explodes one's personal existence. So, many of us, knowing what we should do, refuse to do it.

There is a second reason why white men hesitate to express their goodwill in concrete deeds. This second brake on Christian action in race relations is the danger which such action poses to family and community solidarity. Action produces intergroup as well as intrapersonal tensions. The individual who resolves to eliminate destructive and intolerable tensions in his own soul (those produced by the conflict between his creed and his deed) will quickly discover that his application of an ethical principle to a sore area of society inevitably strains his relation to some members of that society. This danger is present with extraordinary power in areas of interracial friction. The immensity, cruciality, and depth of the racial problem give that problem a divisive force which not only separates the racially different but also estranges those who have divergent views of the problem. Entertain Negroes in your home, take them to dinner with you at the community's finest restaurant, march with them in a demonstration, help them rent or buy a home in a racially exclusive neighborhood, take them with you to church, and "the scandal is there at once." The estranging reaction will range from the ever so slightly raised eyebrow to the open and deliberate effort to drive you out of the community. Some of us have been on the receiving end of both supercilious, curt dismissal and of malicious campaigns aimed at destroying one personally and professionally. However much the offended community may agree with you in principle, it resents your act because you have committed the grave offense of going beyond the community consensus. You have violated a trust, the community's assumption that none of its members will act in any way that embarrasses the others.

Furthermore, your offense has divisive ramifications. It not only alienates you from the group, or from the major part of it; your act sets up divisive tremors through the whole community. For there will be some members of the society who, with the way broken for them, will now do what you have done. The scandal will thus proliferate, lines will be drawn, the issues will be joined, and the community's sweet but deadly peace will be shattered. During my ministry in Charleston, West Virginia, in the late 1950's some of us undertook unsuccessfully to desegregate local hotels and restaurants. With the assistance of one of the aldermen we brought to the city council a proposed ordinance which would have prohibited racial discrimination in public accommodations. Action was required by the fact that the mayor, who had promised to form an interracial committee to work out the problem, had thoughtlessly or deliberately postponed the formation of the committee. The council meeting at which the ordinance was debated proved to be one of the best attended, the most exciting, and the most confused in the city's history. Television cameras, newspaper reporters, and radio microphones covered the heated debates and the testimonies for the ordinance offered by Unitarians, Negroes, Jews, and a lone white Baptist minister. At the height of the excitement one of the aldermen tearfully begged for a postponement of debate and action on the proposed ordinance, saying: "We were a peaceful, happy city until these integrationists tried to get Negroes into our restaurants and hotels. Look at us now, divided, quarreling, a torn and troubled city." Community existence had been exploded by simple acts seeking elemental justice for Charleston Negroes.

Desegregation of Charleston restaurants and hotels was not achieved until many months later and, ironically, after the principals in the council meeting had in various ways passed from the scene. But, to anticipate what must be said in the next chapter, when desegregation finally came it owed its success to a council meeting which had shattered the placidity of the city. But the point here is that action almost invariably produces such community disruptions.

The total picture compels us to note at this point that in facing the problem of racial division Negroes are not exempt from either the intrapersonal or the intergroup tensions which we have been describing. Desegregation, as some Atlanta, Georgia, Negro leaders have confessed, puts Negro motel and restaurant owners in a financial bind which makes them reluctant to champion desegregation. Desegregation throws them into open and unequal competition with white proprietors. For the same reason some Negro realtors, doctors, lawyers, politicians, morticians, and others—failing to rise above their personal interests—resist the breaking up of Negro ghettos in the great metropolitan areas. They fear the scattering of their clients and constituencies and the consequent need to replace the loss from the white community.

Moreover, Negroes have also inherited ideas and concepts about white people, have established social customs which defer to the white man, and, for material security, have accommodated themselves to the white man's structuring of society. Civil rightists are sometimes astonished and depressed by their discovery that some Negroes, having carved out for themselves a comfortable niche in the white man's wall, are apathetic about social change. In addition Negroes find it difficult to resist the urge to find their security within the homogeneous group and must at times face the charge of disloyalty to the Negro race and cause as they make white friends and move into unfamiliar areas of community life. Many years ago a young Negro woman had an apartment in our parsonage. She lived with us for three years, not as a cook or a baby sitter but as a welcomed resident who had her own responsible job elsewhere. Remarkably well adjusted, at home with herself, she was insensitive to the few rebuffs she received in our white, "silk stocking" neighborhood where she was the only Negro. The painful problem which she had to work out was in this instance created not by whites but by Negroes. She had to convince her own racial group that she had not become a traitor to that group by living with white people on a basis of equality. Her act created a small explosion in her own racial community.

Few Christians, white or Negro, want to cause trouble or to be accused of causing trouble even for righteousness' sake. Few Christians relish the blame for shattering the placidity of a cozy, contented community. On the contrary Christians have been taught to avoid conflict, to reconcile people to each other rather than create conflict between them, to seek inner tranquility and peace between men. In the area of housing this problem is particularly acute. There are white Christians who say—and sometimes quite sincerely—that they believe Negroes have the right to buy where they choose and where they are financially able to do so. But these white Christians say: "I have no right to embarrass my neighbor who doesn't feel this way." This can be an excuse for inactivity or it can be a genuine but misguided desire to protect the neighbor. Consequently many Christians, misunderstanding the nature of intrapersonal tension and intergroup conflict, believe that they perform their Christian duty best by keeping quiet and doing nothing. They sanctify their natural desire to stay out of trouble and their laudable desire to maintain communication with other people by convincing themselves that it is their Christian duty *not* to perform the scandalous act and to avoid all racial behavior which incites hostility in their white friends or which strains their family ties. They know what justice and charity demand of them in their relationship to the Negro, but they believe, sometimes earnestly and sometimes as a rationalization, that peace and tranquility are authorities superior to justice and charity.

We have looked at the primary reasons why those Christians who are not vicious bigots, who do have goodwill in their hearts, are confused, baffled, and inactive when confronted by the racial struggle and by the challenge to participate in it. What shall we say to such Christians?

5

Guidelines for Christian Action

The first half of the Swiss slogan to which we referred in the previous chapter—"History is governed by human confusion . . ." —has abundant proof in the racial problems which saturate the whole fabric of the common life and in the bafflement and paralysis of white Christians confronted by those problems. Can white Christians and their churches move from the first part of this Swiss motto into the second and become a part of that history which is governed "by divine providence"? Perhaps, but it will not be easy. William Stringfellow titled his autobiographical polemic of a white lawyer in Harlem *My People Is the Enemy*.[1] He meant white Christians. Can the Negro's enemy become his ally? Can the problem become a part of the solution? If such questions are to have affirmative answers, the answers must be deeds not words.

The time for words has long passed. In fact some deeds are little better than words. Perfunctory acts which work off the tensions of white anxiety, which express pity, which manipulate the destinies of Negroes, which serve the Negro in a condescending spirit and crush his chance to be a man in himself, which make the racial struggle a pool in which the white man dips his soul and washes away his guilt—such acts, even as do words unaccompanied by deeds, widen the chasm between Negroes and whites and compound the problem. What is the Christian mandate and what is the Christian design for action in a racial struggle which moves toward and beyond justice? Let us look then at some guidelines for Christian action in the struggle for racial justice. This series of proposi-

---

1. William Stringfellow, *My People Is the Enemy* (New York: Holt, Rinehart and Winston, 1964).

tions should be likened not to the independent beads on a necklace but to the interrelated sections of a stalk of cane. They are distinct but closely joined propositions.

1. *In the concrete situation Christian love can never be less than justice.* Note that we are dealing here with the concrete situation, with the day by day realities of the racial struggle, and not with speculative philosophical or theological analyses of justice. We are taking Paul Tillich's "ultimately love must satisfy justice in order to be real love, and that justice must be elevated into unity in order to avoid the injustice of eternal destruction" and are applying both of these clauses to such problems as the reorganization of innercity life to free the Negro from domination by the invisible, absentee power-wielders who live far from the metropolitan ghettos. We are applying Emil Brunner's "love can only do more, it can never do less, than justice requires" to housing, votes, jobs. We are accepting Reinhold Niebuhr's dictum that there are therefore "obligations to realize justice in indeterminate degrees" and are not allowing our concern about specific situations to be obfuscated by ultimate and idealistic views of the relation and in some senses the oneness of love and justice. Paul Ramsey is quite correct in stating that "the meaning and measure of full human obligation are to be found only in the biblical conception of righteousness" and in insisting that "the biblical conception of justice . . . requires a great deal more than Aristotle thought was simply just." But however much we need to recover the larger meaning of the word "justice," this is not the sense of the word used today in the concrete situation. Underlying what is said here about justice and later about the love beyond justice are certain presuppositions about the nature of justice, but it is not our task at this point either to define or to defend those presuppositions.[2]

We must also resist here the temptation of another enticing detour—the psychological effect which the white man's refusal to

---

2. For those who are interested in the theoretical aspects of love and justice, minimal reading includes: Paul Tillich, *Love, Power, and Justice* (New York: Oxford University Press, 1954); Emil Brunner, *Justice and the Social Order* (New York: Harper and Row, 1945); Reinhold Niebuhr, *The Nature and Destiny of Man: A Christian Interpretation* (New York: Charles Scribner's Sons, 1943), Vol. II, Ch. IX; Paul Ramsey, *Basic Christian Ethics* (New York: Charles Scribner's Sons, 1950), Ch. I, section 1.

grant justice to the Negro has upon whites themselves. If it is of the essence of justice to treat the other person as a person and if the failure to do so diminishes the personhood of the one who withholds such recognition and such justice—both of these suppositions being psychologically and theologically unassailable—has not the white man marred his own image by sulling that of the Negro? The efforts of the white man to keep the Negro from being fully man—in fact and at times an effort to destroy the Negro personally—have been most costly in the toll they have exacted from the white man as a person. The will to be is always stunted where it does not acknowledge and honor in the other the will to be. An interesting trail, to be sure; but we are now concerned with justice for the Negro, not with the white man's psychic wholeness. We must not be distracted from this present interest by others equally important and intriguing.

With an intuitive wisdom born of long and deeply offended self-interest, the Negro today reduces abstract justice to its tangible forms. He seeks "his"—his rights, his due, his place by his own definitions of himself as a man, a citizen, and a part of the commonalty. He will not be willing to consider the fuller meanings of the word "justice" until he has achieved—in the word's elemental, Aristotelian sense of "to each man his due"—his basic rights. The gradual displacement of the word "integregation" in the Negro protester's vocabulary by such words as "justice," "freedom now," "equal rights," reveals the Negro's willingness to leave questions about intimate Negro-white community to tomorrow and the redemption of the white man's soul to heaven. Predictions that the Negro's rebellion against white domination will temporarily estrange the races from each other are coming true; but the Negro, however much he may regret this inevitable development, cannot let it arrest his struggle for his elemental rights. First things come first and justice has primacy over everything else. And, for the Negro, the word "justice" has specific, practical referents: jobs, housing, health, education, equality with the white man before the law, votes, impartial police protection, desegregated schools, and neighborhood and public facilities of every kind.

Unless white Christians are actually helping Negroes achieve that kind of justice then white Christians' protestations of love for

Negroes must be condemned as specious, even as hypocritical, certainly as ignorant of the elemental meanings of justice and love. As a boy in the South I heard it said over and over that the white Southerner loves the Negro as an individual and the white North-erner loves him as a race. It was thought by Southern whites that this description somehow redounded to the credit of Southerners, proving them more humane than Northerners despite the South's oppression of the Negro. But the facts do not flatter North or South for neither has voluntarily done justice to the Negro; neither has given him his due. By and large Southern whites have loved individual Negroes with the kind of affection one has for a pet or a mentally retarded child and Northern whites have loved the race with a theoretical, detached goodwill. Neither attitude is Christian love and both attitudes, falling short of justice, must fall short of Christian love.

Love and justice are the closest of Siamese twins: the breath and blood of one being sustains and unites them. Love, as Tillich would put it, shows what is just in the particular situation and justice tests love in the given situation. Strictly speaking we cannot say that justice is a foundation on which love stands or that love takes over where justice has finished its work. But for practical purposes it is helpful to think of love and justice as separate func-tions and to visualize them as sequential to each other. Let us consider some illustrations. If love moves the white man toward the Negro and as a result the white man discovers that the Negro—against his will, despite his financial ability to do other-wise, solely because his race is despised—lives in a racial slum dangerous to his mental and physical health, then the white man will do what he can to free the Negro from the curse of the slum or, refusing, will prove that he does not love at all. A white Chris-tian who says that he loves the Negro but who will not help the Negro obtain elemental justice can be compared to an employer who deals with his employee graciously, courteously, kindly, but who refuses to pay the employee his weekly salary. By withholding what by right belongs to the employee and by lavishing on the employee an affection which costs him nothing, the employer des-ecrates both of his relations to his employee—his duty and his affection. As a member of that part of the society which not only refuses to pay the Negro what it owes him but also prevents his achieving on his own initiative what belongs to him, the white Christian who does not in some direct way participate in the struggle for racial justice is either a fool or a hypocrite when he boasts of how much he loves the Negro.

The so-called Golden Rule of Christian ethics—"So whatever you wish that men would do to you, do so to them; for this is the law and the prophets"[3]—does not let us qualify as Christians merely by uttering a few sentiments of affection and compassion. It requires that we "do" and that our doing conform to the demands of an imaginative identification of ourselves with the other man. What would the white Christian want if he were a Negro? What would he want first? He would want justice, his due. He would want all discrimination on the basis of color to end in all areas and levels of society. If his women were seduced by white men, he would want them enabled by the law to receive from the offending white man acknowledgment of parentage and financial support of any children fathered by the white man. Anti-miscegenation laws are unjust and the white Christian who does not seek to remedy this injustice should not prate of Christian love for the Negro. If the racial roles were reversed, the white man would want laws and customs depriving the Negro of the vote overthrown. Nowhere is the Negro's civil estate more crassly and deeply offended than in those areas of the nation where the Negro is deprived of the franchise by local laws, customs, and ingenious devices which keep him from registering and from voting. Justice demands that such denials of suffrage to Negroes cease and no white Christian should babble about love for the Negro so long as he in any way encourages such offenses against the Negro's basic American right or so long as he does not in some way seek for the Negro this right which he himself cherishes as fundamental.

If the white Christian were lifted out of his comfortable, healthy, culturally advantaged, lily-white suburb and set down in a congested, unhealthy, culturally disadvantaged ghetto at the noisy, stinking center of a great industrial metropolis, what would he want? That question answers itself daily as white flee to the suburbs. He would want to get out. And that is what Negroes want.

---

3. Matthew 7:12.

They want to escape from the innercity noose which is strangling them and their children, from the sociological pressure cooker in which they and their children suffocate. They are in many cases economically able to join the flight of those flung by centrifugal psychic and social forces into surrounding suburbs. They are in many cases the social peers and in some cases the moral superiors of suburban residents. They want "out" and they have the will to get out. But they are blocked by racially exclusive neighborhoods. In 1948 in the Shelley v. Kramer case the United States Supreme Court declared that restrictive covenants arrived at by private agreement are not legally binding. But this ruling that neighborhoods cannot be made racially segregated by law did not by law desegregate racially exclusive communities. White segregationists have not exhausted all—indeed, have not tried all—the ways to keep communities racially homogeneous. Restrictive covenants may not be legally binding but they are honored by realtors and by home owners in racially exclusive communities. The city in which I live—Evanston, Illinois—does not exclude Negroes; its population of nearly 80,000 is 12 percent Negro. But through quiet collaboration Evanston realtors and white home owners successfully seclude the city's Negro population in the west-central area of the city. There are a few interracial areas which maintain their racially mixed character and some areas in slow transition from white to Negro, but the major and preferred residential areas of the city are predominantly—some exclusively—white. The exclusion of Negroes from the more attractive, comfortable areas of Evanston continues despite the fact that 57 percent of the city's white population *say* that they would not oppose the desegregation of their communities. The patterns of racial seclusion persist because white home owners and white realtors want them and find within the law ways to preserve them. I have myself examined numerous prospectuses of houses for sale in white neighborhoods in Evanston, each description carefully coded to indicate that the owner reserves the right to restrict the sale of his property. How can a suburban white Christian say with a straight face that he loves and sympathizes with Negroes trapped in the urban ghettos when he does nothing to help Negroes get out of the innercity trap and, for that matter, may be doing all he can to keep the

Negro from getting out? What kind of love is this which deprives the Negro of a basic right—freedom of mobility and settlement? It is, of course, not love at all; for it does not comply with the simple demands of justice.

I have given more time to this illustration than to others for the reason that non-segregated housing is the key to the solution of several other racial problems. Again, take my own city as proof. Fourteen of the city's 20 elementary and junior high schools are more than 80 percent white and five are 100 percent white. Were it not for one Korean student, one of the elementary schools would be 100 percent Negro. Segregation in the Evanston public schools was not contrived. It is a *de facto* segregation, the product of segregated housing. The desegregation of schools, churches, communities, and neighborhood restaurants, libraries, beaches, clubs, does not occur except on a token basis where neighborhoods are exclusively white.

The 1948 Supreme Court decision that restrictive covenants are not legally enforceable was a necessary but inadequate ruling. The Supreme Court had no authority to take the next logical step and compel realtors to offer all houses for sale through them to all interested buyers without regard to race. This move toward what has been called open occupancy must take place through the legislative bodies of states and municipalities. Christians who genuinely believe that they love Negroes with a Christian love and who want to exhibit that love in helping the Negro secure justice must in one way or the other work for open occupancy; for many of the tough, crucial racial problems cannot be solved apart from desegregated housing.

It should not surprise us that Christians, given as they confront the racial problem their option between cheap love and costly justice, choose cheap love. It is of our nature to choose the apparently easy route to a desired destination rather than the obviously hard one. Why not, if both lead to the same goal? Christian love would in fact reach the same end as justice and go beyond that end, for Christian love subsumes justice. But what passes for Christian love for many Christians is not love at all but a mild intoxication derived from infatuation with the idea of love. Love is not love where there occurs no acceptance of the other person's grief, his humiliation, and his hope. Love becomes love in the concrete situation, and in the concrete situation, more often than not, it takes the form of justice.

Let a non-Christian give us a lesson in that kind of love. Erich Fromm in describing *biophilia,* the love of life, states that "love for life will develop most in a society where there is: *security* in the sense that the basic material conditions for a dignified life are not threatened, *justice* in the sense that nobody can be an end for the purposes of another, and *freedom* in the sense that each man has the possibility to be an active and responsible member of society."[4] Does our Christian love want to strike from the Negro the shackles of material deprivation which prevent his having a dignified life and preclude hope that his children will have the dignity he has not had? If so, Christians must transform that love into active justice, for that kind of security—as much the right of the Negro as of the white man—can only be secured through what we call justice. Does our Christian love for the Negro include surrendering him as our robot, as the instrument through which we fulfill ourselves, as the menial, the second-class citizen? If so, Christians must transform that love into specific deeds which in our day extend the Emancipation far more radically, more inclusively, than it was a hundred years ago. The Negro may become one *in* whom we find ourselves but not one by whom we fulfill ourselves. Justice denies the use of a person as a thing. Does our Christian love want the Negro as our peer, our fellow and equal worker as a responsible member of society? We say that we want his help and his cooperation in building a better society, but do we when we consider the challenge of such a Negro to our prestige and our pride? If we do, Christian love must be transformed into just acts; for this means the Negro's election to office, his advancement in the line of promotion, his winning of prizes we have heretofore reserved for whites only.

In 1937 the Oxford Conference of Churches declared: "Undue emphasis upon the higher possibilities of love in personal relations, within the limits of a given system of justice or an established social structure, may tempt Christians to allow individual acts of

---

4. Fromm, *op. cit.,* pp. 52–53.

charity to become a screen for injustice and a substitute for justice." This should be plain enough, but sometimes the obvious truth escapes us. It should have needed no proof that justice has primacy even though it may not have ultimacy in human relations. Micah put justice first and there may be a homily in the sequence in which he summarized what God requires of us. We must do justly before we can love mercy, and both must precede the humble walk with God. Whether the axiom needed demonstration or not, we have now noted at some length what the raw experiences of life teach us every day: in the concrete situation Christian love can never be less than justice.

2. *In the concrete situation justice usually has some form of coercive power for its agent.* We must pause for a moment on the word "usually." For it has become the vogue with civil rights workers to say that the white man never voluntarily does justice to the Negro, that he never gives the Negro his rights unless he is compelled to do so. This derogatory generalization about white men—in turn, a generalization about all men—ignores the facts; it will not stand up under the easy historical tests we can apply to it. One solid example is enough to show how careless of facts such uses of the word "never" are. As early as 1671 George Fox urged his Quaker followers to teach their Negroes Christianity, use them gently, and after a time free them. It took a hundred years but by 1770 Quakers were refusing to participate in the slave trade. Six years later the Quakers, even in the South, outlawed slave-owning among their members. "In 1776 the North Carolina Society of Friends took its first definite step toward emancipation. The Yearly Meeting advised its members 'to cleanse their hands of slaves as soon as they possibly can' and resolved that 'any member of this meeting who may hereafter buy, sell or clandestinely assign for hire any slave in such manner as may perpetuate or prolong their slavery' should be disowned."[5] These were white men who voluntarily sought justice for the Negro and who did so moved by no outward power but solely by an inner compulsion. They did not act because they were coerced into doing so. The reverse was true.

5. Johnson, *op. cit.*, p. 460.

The Quakers voluntarily freed their slaves in opposition to the powers which ruled their day. If there were no others, the Quakers alone would be enough to redeem white men from the general curse that they are never moved by goodwill to do justly. But, to be truthful, many white men have as individuals voluntarily lifted the Negro. In the long run it does the Negro's cause no good to rewrite history and bury the fact that the Negro in his escape from slavery and his move toward equality has been and is the beneficiary of white champions who have acted solely from goodwill. It is not only inaccurate but also unjust and a foolish foreclosure of one avenue of racial progress to say that goodwill and persuasion never produce results.

Still, the hard fact remains: justice must usually have some form of coercive power as its agent. This truism rests first on the natural unwillingness of men to relinquish their advantage over each other voluntarily. The voluntary adjustment does happen but much too infrequently to solve massive social problems. Consider for example the general deterioration of the Negro's condition following Booker T. Washington's "Atlanta Compromise" address at the Cotton States Exposition on September 18, 1895. In this masterfully subtle address Washington sought to cajole white Southerners. Speaking for Negroes as he alone at that time spoke for Negroes, he surrendered his people's political ambitions, their civil rights, and their claim on any education other than agricultural and industrial training. He did so because he believed as he said later in *Up from Slavery*, that, "Just as soon as the South gets over the old feeling that it is being forced by 'foreigners,' or 'aliens,' to do something which it does not want to do, I believe that the change in the direction I have indicated [the rallying of the South to the Negro's cause] is going to begin. In fact there are indications that it is already beginning in a slight degree."[6] W. E. B. Du Bois in his *The Souls of Black Folk* claimed that Booker T. Washington's reliance upon persuasion was a major contributor to several catastrophes which befell the Negro in the 15 years following the Atlanta Exposition: "the disfranchisement of the Negro, the legal creation of a distinct status of civil inferiority for the Negro,

---

6. Booker T. Washington, *Up from Slavery* (Garden City, N.Y.: The Sun Dial Press, 1937), pp. 234–235. (Originally published by Doubleday & Company, Inc.)

and the steady withdrawal of aid from institutions for the higher
training of Negroes."[7]

The techniques of Martin Luther King, Jr., in his programs of
non-violent, direct action are in instructive contrast to those of
Booker T. Washington. Both men could be called non-violent, but
King does not rely upon persuasion, not even on Gandhian passive
resistance. There is always an element of coercion in King's protests. The forces he employs are sometimes subtle, sometimes implied, sometimes open, but always present. Nowhere in his program do we find a pacifistic renunciation of force as an instrument.
He insists only that the force he and his followers employ not be
violent or merely retaliatory. In the Montgomery, Alabama, bus
boycott King learned that where moral imperatives and economic
pressures converge upon racial justice the white man can be compelled to act. Sometimes, as in the demonstrations seeking the
registration of Negroes in Selma, Alabama, King applies pressure
on two levels: on the local level seeking the immediate solution of
a specific and limited problem and on the national level seeking
federal government action which can be applied over a broad area.
Moreover where Booker T. Washington surrendered much in the
hope of gaining a little, Martin Luther King, Jr., concedes nothing.
He does not bargain with the white man; he does not say, "If you
will give us this, we will not ask for that." He claims the whole
range of human rights for Negroes, but as a tactical stroke concentrates the power of his movement where the Negro is strongest and
the white man's resistance most vulnerable. King's reliance upon
non-violent coercion—and various modifications of his form of
protest—succeeds; Washington's reliance upon persuasion and his
appeal to the conscience of the white man failed.

It can not be concluded that, since persuasion and sentimental
appeals to the nation's political and religious creeds will not secure
racial justice in the United States, violent applications of naked
force will. We need not conclude that the repudiation of one extreme drives us to embrace the other. The use of force in the
protest against racial injustice in the United States does not anticipate or require a bloody revolution. No doubt the Negro—if there

---

7. W. E. B. Du Bois, *The Souls of Black Folk* (Chicago: A. C. McClurg and
Company, 1920), p. 51.

were unanimous dedication to such a revolution—could by the use of brute force create widespread confusion and disorder. Terrorists like those arrested by New York City police and the Federal Bureau of Investigation and charged with plotting to blow up the Statue of Liberty, the Washington Monument, and the Liberty Bell are considered fools by most Negroes and will gather few followers. But they can disrupt the nation and, unfortunately, can in some minds discredit the Negro's struggle for his rights. The violence which has in recent years erupted in Brooklyn in physical attacks on the police, the destruction of property, and the terrorizing of innocent bystanders could paralyze city life if it becomes widespread. The Negro's deep moral and civil loyalties—so long as his protest makes progress—are guarantees that he will not choose violence as the way toward justice for his people. Moreover, despite what some extremist Negro leaders say, there is among Negroes no widespread, bitter hatred of the white man. It would not be surprising if rancor ruled the Negro's conduct in his relation with the white man, but there is no evidence that Negroes generally have surrendered all hopes for the peaceful accommodation of the races to each other.

The Negro's rejection of massive, total revolution as a way out of the social trap rises also from his prudence. He knows that he is up against a superior numerical and material power and he has reason to fear that if the battle descends to that level what Sir Harry Johnston said of the white man will prove true: "There is sufficient of the devil still left in the white man for the 300 years' cruelties of Negro slavery to be repeated, if it were worth the white man's while."[8] And, we might add, if the white man is given a sufficient excuse. Despite the threat implicit in James Baldwin's *The Fire Next Time,* despite occasional episodes of guerrilla warfare, despite deliberate efforts by whites to provoke Negroes to a suicidal violence, the Negro will not take this road from where he is to where he should be. No responsible, influential Negro leader suggests even by implication that the Negro should take up arms against the white man. It can be concluded that when the racial struggle on the American scene relies solely upon persuasion or

---

8. Kelly Miller, *Out of the House of Bondage* (New York: Neele Publishing Company, 1914), p. 15.

exclusively upon violent rebellion it will fail. It will succeed to the extent that the leaders of the struggle—Negro and white—gauge correctly what mixture of non-violence and coercion the concrete situation demands. The power which Negroes and whites must employ in achieving a truly full, democratic society must be non-violent, coercive direct action. Therefore the question is not one of how to use brute force but how to employ legal, economic, psychological pressures to secure social change.

Second, the psychological justifications for the use of coercive power in the racial struggle should not be ignored or underestimated. If the Negro does not add pressure to his plea the white man will conclude that the Negro is not in earnest. He will assume as many white men until recently did in the Deep South that Negroes are contented with things as they are. For generations Negroes asked for justice hat-in-hand and the white man paid them no attention. The white South was wildly enthusiastic in receiving Washington's "Atlanta Compromise"—"The fairest women of Georgia stood up and cheered," said the *New York World* correspondent James Creelman, in his report of Washington's speech—because Washington claimed so little for the Negro and threatened not at all. He let the South believe that the Negro wanted only a token and would cause no trouble to get that. So they listened to him rather than to those Negroes who were insulted by the concessions he made. Washington—half-white and half-Negro—could never bring pressure against one of his races for the sake of the other.

W. E. B. Du Bois—proud of his French and Dutch as well as his Negro ancestry—found his identity as a Negro and incessantly pressed the white man for justice. He saw and labeled Washington's fatal error: "His doctrine had tended to make the whites, North and South, shift the burden of the Negro problem to the Negro's shoulder and stand aside as critical and rather pessimistic spectators; when in fact the burden belongs to the nation, and the hands of none of us are clean if we bend not our energies to righting these great wrongs."[9] Du Bois read human nature deeper than Washington. He knew that it was futile for the Negro to trust his welfare to the white man and that his protests would not be

9. Du Bois, *op. cit.*, p. 58.

valid unless they in some way involved the white man's self-interest.

There is another reason why the psychology of human nature demands forceful action in the racial protest. When a white man takes a firm public stand against some form of desegregation or when he sincerely believes that desegregation violates his religion, he may have a change of mind and want to comply with changing circumstances but he cannot do so and at the same time retain his self-respect and his sense of dignity. He has gone too far to go back, unless he can claim that he has been forced to. Many a racist has given in where he has boasted he would never comply with changing racial patterns because he has been able to blame his surrender on the United States Supreme Court or on the financial ruin which would result from continued resistance. There have even been instances in which racists seem to be saying to threatening changes in racial customs: "I know what you demand is right; make me do it." In many cases segregationists have deserted their boastful defiance of all change not because the force brought against them was overpowering but because it removed from them the onus of compliance with a way of life distasteful to them and abhorrent to the memory of revered ancestors.

Third, the use of coercive power in the search for racial justice is required by the fact that racial injustice is deeply entrenched in and massively fortified by the nation's social structures. We have already noticed that the power structures in American life are directly and indirectly responsible for ostracizing and exploiting the Negro. Through his control of education, employment, housing, the law, politics, the nation's financial life, the churches, government, law enforcement—in a word, all of the nation's instrumentalities—the white man suppressed the Negro and thwarted his rise to first-class citizenship. Since the white man has at his control and disposal the agencies of the social order, he can continue to suppress and thwart the Negro without apparent intention or effort to do so. By making the repression of the Negro a part of the social and civil systems he can perpetuate the most humiliating forms of injustice while throwing upon the Negro the ordeal and onus of overthrowing the existing situation. Where segregation and discrimination are written into the law—as they are in the South—

the white man can retain his unjust advantage over the Negro as a defender of the law, compelling the Negro to become—as in such situations he must—the breaker of the law. The white man's power over the Negro—established in regional law—must be challenged by appeals to a higher law and this can often only be done by violations of local law. Such challenges leave the impression that the Negro resorts to force and that the white man does not. But this impression does not describe the situation accurately. When the Negro, operating within the bounds of his Constitutional right, defies local authorities and violates unjust local laws he in fact counters an oppressive hidden force with a rebellious open force. The cycle of force begins with the white man—with his law and his police force. The Negro's action is in effect a delayed reaction to those earlier, oppressive acts through which the white man developed a social order which degrades and humiliates the Negro. The Negro, ground down by a law which was devised to imprison him in a social substratum, must defy the law fashioned to oppress him and must do so whatever the light in which it makes him appear.

Where these are the conditions, white Christians who condemn the Negro for breaking the law can be assumed more interested in oppressive order and humiliating peace than they are in justice. Indeed, if white Christians are interested in fulfilling love's demand for justice they will champion and aid the Negro in his breaking of those laws which deprive him of his rights. They will see with what tremendous odds the Negro must contend in bringing what pressure he can against the forces of injustice which bind and strangle him. They will seek to restore the balance of power, throwing their weight and the weight of those agencies they control or influence on the side of the oppressed rather than that of the oppressor. They will not by silence and inactivity imply that all laws—even flagrantly unjust ones—are sacred, but will insist that the rights of men are sacred and that laws which offend those rights are evil and must not be obeyed. If it is argued that the violation of unjust laws produces a contempt for all laws—an argument in which there is some truth—let white Christians remember that contempt for the law begins in this case with the white man's unjust law not with contemptuous Negroes. It cannot be expected that oppressive laws

will produce law-abiding citizens. Nor can it be expected that Negroes who have suffered unjustly under the law will forever prefer
the rectifying processes of legal appeal to a higher law.

In parts of the country other than the South the white man's
hidden control over the social and civil destinies of the Negro
takes other forms than deliberately oppressive laws. When Negroes
were unable to buy homes in exclusively white Deerfield, Illinois,
Negroes and white integrationists sought to purchase land on
which to build non-segregated housing. The local government, ex-
ercising the right of eminent domain, appropriated the property
selected by the integregationists and thus prevented the entry of
Negroes into Deerfield. A just law was apparently applied unjustly
and in a manner which made it impossible for the village government's ulterior motive to be exposed or its action to be challenged
legally. Such tactics are merely one of the numerous subterfuges
open to whites in their exclusion of Negroes where the whites
control the local government.

Extralegal methods of excluding the Negro from residential
areas, professions, unions, clubs, schools, colleges, management,
and other appendages of the white-dominated power structures are
often more subtle but no less effective than legal and illegal methods. Although the federal government makes it increasingly difficult for the home-building industry to discriminate against minority groups where the federal government participates in any way in
the financing of housing projects, independent home-builders, in
collusion with the controllers of mortgage credit, can prevent the
desegregation of neighborhoods. A Cleveland banker stated pub-
licly: "We do not finance the first Negro purchaser in a white area
for public reasons. White resentment in the area would be great,
probably resulting in account cancellations and discontinuance of
other business."[10] With few exceptions the white man's covert
power determines where the Negro lives. Since the purpose of that
kind of power is to exclude the Negro it obviously cannot be
dissipated by patience and persuasion. The Negro must counter the
racists' conservative power with coercive power; he must interject
into what is for him an oppressively static situation such dynamic

10. Davis McEntire, *Residence and Race* (Los Angeles: University of California
Press, 1960), p. 225.

actions as will disrupt the white community's inertness and make change a possibility.

Through the use of various devices the white man has systematically excluded the Negro from the nation's economic structure. There have been notable and sometimes dramatic improvements in the Negro's place in the country's economy since Simpson and Yinger made their monumental study of racial and cultural minorities 12 years ago.[11] But the conditions, while improved, remain generally the same; and the white man still resists the rise of the Negro in trade unions, the medical field, the legal profession, banking, and related professions. As the white man has used his power, sometimes openly and ruthlessly, sometimes subtly and genteelly but equally ruthlessly, to keep the Negro out of his segregated neighborhoods, so too he has excluded the Negro from the great white belt of the national economy. The number of Negroes who are competent in native ability and training to enter these heretofore forbidden areas of the nation's economy increases faster than qualified Negroes are absorbed. Thus pressures of frustration and resentment rise in the Negro community and these pressures find expression in various forms of vigorous protest. The frustrated Negro, trained for jobs and professions from which he is barred solely by his race, is baffled further by his inability to locate the enemy, the oppressor, in a visible and vulnerable form. So he strikes out against "the man," against white society in general. And this may be as good a target as any since it is entrenched white society in general which excludes him and denies him those duties and privileges for which he has qualified.

In a word, then, the Negro is the victim of both an open and a hidden white power which assumes many repressive forms. That power—which works for racial injustice—is ancient, legalized, implicit in the nation's social and economic systems, disguised as peace and order, countenanced by a religion which honors peace more than it does justice and which profits from the repressive power it tacitly endorses. Against such power, patience and persuasion are helpless. If the Negro is to obtain justice, he and the whites who struggle by his side for a just society must use those

---

11. George Eaton Simpson and S. Milton Yinger, *Racial and Cultural Minorities* (New York: Harper and Row, 1953), Part Two.

coercive powers which can be honored not only by their goal but also by their standards of ethical means and by their quest for human dignity. White Christians, by the very nature of the concrete human situation, cannot escape direct involvement in the power struggle. Nor can they avoid the use of power. By being in the situation they will throw their weight either on the side of a restrictive power which preserves the unjust status quo or on the side of a coercive power which disrupts the status quo and makes justice an option in human relations. To say as does Carl F. H. Henry, editor of *Christianity Today,* that "Christianity promotes neither a just coerced society nor a free unjust society" is not merely to profane the gospel but also is in fact to give aid and comfort to the fashioners of an unjust society. Henry and the great masses of nominal Christians who share his views fall willingly into the trap so plainly labeled by Pascal: "Because men do not fortify justice, they justify force." One way or the other Christians participate in the power struggle and are the wielders of power. They either side with the poor, the downtrodden, the oppressed, the weak, or they take up arms against them.

3. *Conflict is inherent in the concrete human situation.* All human relations have conflict—hidden or open, dormant or active—as a principal factor. This fact can be simply stated but its products are neither few nor simple. While on the one hand our acceptance of conflict's inevitability provides correctives for naïve assumptions about society, on the other hand this premise is one from which erroneous and dangerous conclusions can be drawn. We must therefore examine the complexities of this elemental statement as they appear in the struggle for racial justice. We begin by giving some supports to the premise that conflict can be expected wherever and however we meet the racial problem. This statement about the ubiquity of conflict requires that conflict be defined not only as open hostility and competition but also as psychic and concealed antagonisms. Lewis A. Coser, in an illustration drawn appropriately from the racial struggle, uses the word "conflict" in a strictly sociological sense: "To take a concrete illustration: it would be imprudent to conclude from the absence of conflict in race relations that there is interracial adjustment. The

lack of conflict between Negroes and whites in the South, in contrast to frequent conflicts in race relations in many a Northern city, has often been taken to indicate that Negro-white relations are more stable in the South. Such a conclusion appears to be unjustified. The absence of conflict in itself does not indicate absence of feelings of hostility and antagonism and hence absence of elements of strain and malintegration."[12] We, however, shall use the term in its more inclusive sense.

The Christian by definition is never a deliberate troublemaker, never sows seeds of suspicion, never does the ethical act simply for effect. His purpose is not to shock people, to coerce them, or to create conflict where conflict does not already exist. His purpose is justice, charity, reconciliation. But by the very nature of the human situation there are times when these three are not mutually inclusive. Consider, first, the fact that the silence and inactivity which purchase the white man's peace with his family and his white friends and neighbors offends Negroes and alienates him from them. One way or the other, active in racial goodwill or inactive, he participates in a basic human conflict. If he says and does nothing to aid the oppressed and humiliated Negro, there is tension between him and the Negro. If he acts in justice and charity, there is tension between him and white people irritated by his action. He therefore cannot decide what he should do on a conflict-or-no-conflict basis. He must decide his course on the basis of what he concludes is God's will for him in the situation and let conflict express itself as it will. What he does will hurt someone, antagonize someone. The Christian in the life-situation does not choose one human conflict over another; he chooses the deed which he believes God wills for him and lets the conflict choose him.

It is quite obvious that society's tranquilizers can keep the tensions created by the racial problem temporarily submerged and subdued. Such soporifics as gentility, courtesy, supine surrender to custom, hunger for acceptance, the desire to please and reluctance to offend—these lull white man and Negro into hypocritical pretenses of concord. But the conflicts remain nevertheless. In the

---

12. Lewis A. Coser, *The Function of Social Conflict* (Glencoe, Ill.: The Free Press, 1956), p. 82.

typical Mississippi town the clash of hopes and fears in Negro town and white town occurs beneath the surface as the white man assures himself that "our Negroes like it this way" and as the Negro, powerless or intimidated, accepts at least outwardly the white man's myth about Negro contentment. There is no apparent tension in such a situation. Then comes the incident—the refusal of a Negro to sit in the back of a bus, the sit-in at the local lunch counter, the coming of a white freedom rider, the appearance of a registered Negro voter at the polls, a white minister's declaration that the gospel is on the side of the Negro. The seemingly innocuous act explodes an apparently placid community. It does so—not as the white man says because some outsiders have come and stirred up the Negro—because the incident is a short fuse leading to huge deposits of suspicion, fear, hatred, and resentment many years buried but now ready to explode.

If it is true that conflict is inherent in the human situation, then it is not true as some reformers contend that conflict has to be induced between peoples in order to achieve desired social benefits. One of the popular views of community organization and development today holds that desired reforms can only be achieved by intensifying and if necessary creating frictions in the community, by polarizing the forces operating in the community, and by giving the community a visible and vulnerable Enemy which it can attack. In a *Christian Century* article published January 22, 1964, William W. Biddle, of the United Presbyterian Board of National Missions, rebuked Christian crusaders who assume "that human beings will not become active in righteous causes unless they are stirred to struggle against identified enemies —an imitation of the 'good guys vs. bad guys' theme celebrated interminably in movies and television." Biddle recognizes the probability of conflict. He knows that rivalry, tension, and hostility are factors in the human situation. Consequently he knows that they do not have to be produced or heightened in order to achieve those creative tensions which result from contending interests and which, if properly managed, can produce social progress.

Some stress should be put on the words "can produce" in the closing sentence of the preceding paragraph. It is idle to suppose that human conflict of itself necessarily produces social progress.

In the work noted above, Coser quotes Alfred North Whitehead's dictum: "The clash of doctrines is not a disaster, it is an opportunity." The clash of interests in any given social context is also an opportunity, but nothing better than that. Conflict can be and often is tragically destructive and it is always destructive when it becomes an end in itself. These words are written two days following the assassination of Malcolm X, the Black Nationalist leader who deserted Elijah Muhammad, leader of the Black Muslim movement. They are written on the day fire swept the Black Muslim headquarters in Harlem in what was apparently retaliation for the murder of Malcolm X. The papers are full of reports that followers of the assassinated Negro plan to execute Black Muslim leaders. This is a pat illustration of what happens when human conflict runs amuck. We must return to this thought near the close of this chapter when we consider how Christian concern moves beyond justice. For the present we are saying that conflict should neither be abhorred nor cherished in itself but should be treated as an opportunity for social progress.

We can conclude, however, that open social conflict is more healthful, more productive of social progress than hidden tensions. One of the roles of the ethical act, in whatever field and however bold and unconventional, is to transform hidden conflict which cannot be resolved into open conflict which can be made creative. The ethical act, contrary to what timid Christians suppose, does not in fact produce conflict. On the contrary the deed is a "scandal" in that it exposes tensions which already exist. The act threatens us because it strips away the formalities, the convivial screens of conversational and fashionable pleasantries, and reveals the ugliness we thought we alone knew hidden in us. The act shatters the pretenses of amiability and agreement between men, behind which hide clashing racial opinions and conflicting racial moods. The act, in other words, explodes artificial existence by exposing the concealed conflicts which are inherent in all vital social issues. For example a Christian minister may Sunday after Sunday preach brotherhood, justice, and charity in vague generalities and in a setting where such preaching is expected, without causing a ripple in his congregation. His ideas and those of the racists in his congregation may be incompatible, but there develops between him and them a tacit gentlemen's agreement which lets him say what he wants to and permits them to go on living as they please. But if the minister acts—joins the National Association for the Advancement of Colored People; heads a committee to open segregated schools, restaurants, playgrounds, housing; aids Negroes in registering and in going to the polls; invites Negroes to join the church—his act uncovers the hidden conflicts. By disclosing what has been present but hidden his act brings buried but nonetheless insidious tensions into the open where they can be confronted and made creative. We conclude, then, that the ethical act in the area of racial goodwill does not create tensions; rather it discloses already existing tensions and by disclosing them makes them potentially creative. Open conflict, as Coser put it, "eliminates the accumulation of blocked and balked hostile dispositions by allowing their free behavioral expression."[13]

The transformation of covert conflict into open conflict occurs under two circumstances, one of which is more creative than the other. First, conflict rises to the surface—becomes potentially physical and violent—where its repression can no longer be tolerated. Unfortunately this is the condition under which the Negro has usually had to expose his bitterness, his resentment, and his hostility. He has done so explosively when the repression of those feelings was no longer a live option, when he could no longer endure the pressures of injustice and frustration. Second, conflict can be exposed and made creative where it is assumed that the human relationship has such solidarity that it will not be destroyed by the revealed hostility. Unfortunately this is the condition which white Christians have stubbornly refused to produce.

Whatever the circumstances under which hidden conflict is exposed, the white Christian should understand that repressed hostility is much more destructive of human values than exposed conflicts. The first condition is poisonous; the second, potentially healthful. The first is static; the second, dynamic. In the first there is no possible cure for the white man's guilt or the Negro's oppression; in the second there is opportunity for a creative redemption of the white man and a fruitful release of the Negro. What the white man commonly calls racial peace means desola-

13. *Ibid.*, p. 39.

tion to the Negro. What the white man commonly and often mistakenly calls racial trouble may indeed sometimes be a dangerous disorder. But more often than not open racial conflict must be precipitated by an incident, an act, if men are to know themselves, each other, and the true nature of the conflict and if together they are to achieve solutions of the psychological and social problems. The ethical act, therefore, the unconventional racial deed which cuts across accepted social patterns, is indispensable if the white man's soul and the Negro's whole life are to be rescued from the perils of racial prejudice and discrimination.

We begin to see, then, the paradoxical nature of tension in the field of race relations. It is always inherent in the human situation and particularly in the areas of ethnic prejudice and exploitation. Neither this tension nor resulting hostility has to be artificially produced in order to rouse Negroes to protest against the abuse of their people or to muster white men to champion justice and charity. But the ethical act—which must always be meritorious in itself—serves as a catalyst, stimulating in a stagnant and toxic racial situation a remedial and constructive reaction. The stiff demands of justice and love require the act for the act's sake; but love and justice demonstrated in a deed unsettle complacent communities, break up caked minds, dislodge comfortable spirits, helping to provide that ripeness of time in which a new day may emerge for white man and Negro. The enemies we fear most, the ones which paralyze us—tension and conflict—prove when exposed and used creatively, to be the allies of a just and charitable society.

4. *In the concrete human situation Christian action sometimes has unfortunate by-products.* It would be a fair world indeed— perhaps also a dull one—if all ethical acts were by their virtue and their good intentions guaranteed against the production of unhappy consequences. That, however, is not the kind of world we live in. On the contrary the good deed—always subject to misunderstanding and to deliberate distortion—can produce harmful as well as beneficial effects. We are thinking now of something more than the penalty which men of action pay for their good deeds. That good men suffer more than anyone else from the harmful side-

effects of their own good deeds must be one of the best attested facts of human history. And their suffering is compounded by their awareness that others must help pay the price of their act and that some will be the reluctant or the innocent victims of the irony which often mocks man's noblest purposes. This is man's condition: his best acts sometimes have unhappy consequences and his noblest achievements have unfortunate companions.

No one in secular literature has ever confronted and expressed the harshness of the human option more boldly and truthfully than did Lincoln in his Second Inaugural. As a Southerner and as one whose family had inherited even in the third generation some of the deprivations produced in the South by the Civil War, I shall never forget with what horror, what repugnance, I first read those Inaugural words which, as I recall, are perpetuated in the Lincoln Memorial in Washington: "Fondly do we hope, fervently do we pray, that this mighty scourge of war may speedily pass away. Yet, if God wills that it continue until all the wealth piled by the bondsman's two hundred and fifty years of unrequited toil shall be sunk, and until every drop of blood drawn with the lash shall be paid by another drawn with the sword, as was said three thousand years ago, so still it must be said, 'The judgments of the Lord are true and righteous altogether.' " There is large ground for concluding that the war should never have occurred, that either North or South could have prevented it. But when these words were spoken deep in the Civil War's fourth year they defined in prophetic tones the terror and the tribulation which accompanied Lincoln's resolve to preserve the union and to emancipate the slaves. On both sides of the battle exorbitant prices were exacted by Lincoln's resolute pursuit of worthy ends. At that juncture in history Lincoln could neither cease nor continue without causing great suffering on both sides of the battle line. Specifically he could not do what he believed God was requiring of him in the situation without producing results which he viewed as tragic. The pure act was impossible.

In our own day the racial struggle remains among all the others the most conclusive proof that good deeds usually have tragic by-products. When Martin Luther King, Jr., launched demonstrations to secure voting rights for Negroes in Selma, Alabama, his motivation, his goal, and his method all conformed to the highest qualifications of Christian purpose and Christian ethics. This, however, did not preclude all unfortunate consequences. Unitarian minister James J. Reeb was beaten to death by brutal racists in Selma, and Mrs. Viola Gregg Liuzzo was shot to death during the march from Selma to Montgomery. In addition to the sacrificial yet ironic death of these two white civil rightists other white people and numerous Negroes suffered in their bodies the cruel assaults of vicious hatred. It was almost inevitable from the beginning of this protest that many should suffer and that some should die. It can be expected that similar demonstrations will provide the occasions in which similar tragedies occur. This is a part of the price which must be paid for the uprooting of deeply anchored racial injustice.

These two dramatic events illustrate a rule of life which applies not only to those epochal histories which affect great masses of people but also to the obscure individual's lone and largely unnoticed act of goodwill. His act, too, is in some respects a gamble. He can be sure that his deed—however carefully planned, prayerfully executed, nobly dedicated—will not produce an unalloyed result. If he acts as an ethically responsible person, there will be blessings for someone but there will also be attendant sorrows. Think, for example, of the young men and women who have reluctantly but deliberately broken family ties by openly rejecting the racial bigotries taught them by their parents from childhood. By no amount of tact can they combine faithfulness and harmlessness. They act as they must act and some of the consequences are tragic. Or think of those ministers who because of a racial crisis in their parish or somewhere else in the country must speak and act in ways that may separate them from their people. I can testify out of 23 years in the parish ministry that few things pain a sensitive pastor more than estrangement from his people. Yet there are times when loyalties higher than those he owes to the people require deeds which may alienate him from the people. Usually in such situations he has neither the time nor the ability to weigh the potential harm against the probable good, no time for nor interest in the prudential decision. He does what he believes the situation requires and suffers whatever injuries his faithfulness may produce in him or in those who may be his act's innocent victims.

Let us return for a moment to our reference to legitimate protests against racial injustice and to the harmful by-products of such acts. Since such coercive demonstrations are likely to occur now in any community in the United States, it is well to understand not only the good which they seek and accomplish but also the evil which, like camp-followers, clings to them. (And let it be known that we seek such understanding not as an exemption from the racial struggle but as a solid ground for deep involvement.) The more massive and dramatic the demonstration the greater the probability that it will attract people who view it as a lark, as an end in itself, or as an opportunity to vent long repressed vengefulness. Thus far the Negro protester's constancy in his faithfulness to principles and policies of non-violent demonstration has been so incredible as to require new chapters in the history of man's peaceful struggle for freedom and equality.

But we cannot expect such patience and such discipline to continue unbroken as in the last throes of the racial struggle the Negro's "Now!" collides North and South with the white racist's "Never!" We cannot expect that the Negro will forever be shot down, clubbed, gassed, and bombed without protecting himself physically and without retaliating in kind. We cannot expect that the Martin Luther Kings will always be able to contend with the white man with one peaceful hand and successfully restrain Negroes committed to violent action with the other. Nor can we assume that the ranks of demonstrators will remain free of those who are irresponsible troubleseekers or who see in demonstrations an opportunity to release long restrained hostilities. Though the leaders of racial protests of all kinds should do their best to weed out potential troublemakers who will subvert the purposes of protest, such screenings cannot always be successful. Moreover, once a protest gets under way it attracts followers who may not necessarily share its philosophy or its disciplines. In any event, as the saying has it, revolutions are never tidy affairs. The racial struggle, approaching in the second half of the twentieth century the dimensions of a revolution, will inevitably leave some human wreckage in its wake. No social, national, or religious venture today commends itself so highly to the Christian conscience as does the current struggle for freedom and equality for the American Negro. None has so certainly the Christian mandate for action. Yet however skillfully the struggle is managed, it will in the nature of the case have unfortunate by-products. The pure act is impossible.

This fact causes trouble for the shallow-thinking idealist. A story out of Memphis, Tennessee, illustrates how idealistic men of goodwill, waiting for the pure act, fail to become deeply involved in the struggle for racial justice. An editorial in *The Commercial Appeal,* a Memphis, Tennessee, newspaper, lauded the Reverend James Madison Barr, minister of the Memphis First Unitarian Church, for his attitudes on the tragic death of another Unitarian minister, the Reverend James J. Reeb, the Boston clergyman beaten to death in Selma, Alabama, by white racists. *The Commercial Appeal* in an April 15, 1965, news report stated: "The minister of First Unitarian Church here said yesterday responsibility for the death of a Unitarian minister at Selma, Ala., must rest with Rev. Martin Luther King along with the men who 'brutally beat Jim Reeb' to death. Jim Reeb died because he went to Selma, Ala. . . . And the city of Selma would not have been visited by Jim Reeb save for the demonstrations set up and planned here by Martin Luther King and COFO." The Memphis minister condemned hatred and violence and called for integrated schools and an "open door policy in Memphis." Yet he blamed King for the murder of Reeb. Let us suppose that the members of Mr. Barr's church take him seriously and try in non-violent deeds as well as words to break open Memphis' racially closed society. If they do, if they act for justice and some of them are treated violently or perhaps killed, will Mr. Barr consider himself guilty of violence and murder? Will he share the blame with those who hate and kill? No, in that case he would not let himself be trapped by the spurious logic with which he condemns Martin Luther King, Jr.

Racists, not above using terroristic methods themselves, are quick to point out to those who act in the Negro's behalf that such action may have harmful results. Indeed, they employ terror as much for its indirect as for its direct effect. The primary purpose of a bombing or beating of Negroes and whites is not to eliminate a particular Negro or white integregationist but to create in sensitive civil rightists a revulsion for actions which trigger such brutal retaliation. They may not have thought the matter through but a part of the racists' mixed subconscious purpose is to make the by-product of the ethical act so horrible that the act itself will be surrendered. Racists who would not stoop to terroristic acts themselves share this hope. Their twisted logic encourages the trust that savagery in sufficient quantity will convince integrationists that their attacks on the South's closed society are doing more harm than good. Civil rightists have long been far too sophisticated and much too resolute to be deterred either by such spurious logic or by their painful awareness that some people must pay a dearer price for their actions than they pay themselves.

Enlightened civil rights workers know, for one thing, that in crass hypocrisy segregationists often hide a contempt for one people beneath a profuse concern for another. In the April 1, 1965, issue of the *Georgia Bulletin,* a Roman Catholic diocesan newspaper, there appeared a probable illustration of this kind of sentimental duplicity. After Archbishop Paul J. Hallinan permitted his priests to participate in the Selma, Alabama, voting rights demonstration he received numerous favorable and unfavorable letters commenting on his decision. Among the excerpts from these letters published in the "Archbishop's Notebook" in the *Georgia Bulletin* was one which read: "I do not see how you can justify your action in exposing our gentle nuns to possible physical harm and to words and actions they could not comprehend." Though there were no nuns from the Atlanta archdiocese in Selma, the complaint illustrates the point. From the tone and context of the rebuke we can infer that the writer was provoked not by the exposure of nuns to danger but by their exposure for a cause he found repugnant. A profuse concern for the safety of nuns concealed an indifference about the welfare of Negroes.

When King proposed a boycott of Alabama the state's administrative officials suddenly became greatly concerned about the effects of a boycott on Alabama's poor Negroes. With eyes full of crocodile tears they denounced the proposal as a cruel blow to the innocent white people and to the Negroes of the state. How, the state officials asked, can King, a professing Christian, be so indifferent, so insensitive to the feelings and the welfare of his own people? This sudden concern for Negroes condemns itself. Where were these new champions of Alabama Negroes when the Negroes were beaten, bombed, murdered, by whites? Where have they been during the long years in which Negroes have endured in Alabama a servitude little better than slavery? Why this quick conversion? Obviously, these white officials are not really concerned about the welfare of the Negro but about their own pocketbooks. They use the vulnerability of Alabama's Negroes as a pawn to block attacks on white supremacy in their state.

Responsible men do not pursue good ends in blithe indifference and insensitivity to the harmful by-products of their good deeds. In the thick of the crucial human struggles they can take no pride in their brave good deeds, for they know that others along with them must pay a dear price for every ethical act they perform. But neither do they permit themselves to be muted and paralyzed by the coincidental tragedies and misfortunes which shadow all human actions, both good and evil. The first time I used in print Wilberforce's identification of himself with the whole tragedy of racial injustice I thought it a grand, idealistic aspiration. But he meant more than that when he said, "I mean not to accuse anyone, but to take the shame upon myself in common with the whole of my people." The just act can be cruel if it views indifferently the innocent and the uncommitted people it sucks into the wake of its sacrifices and its sorrows. The actor must be willing to take upon himself the shame and into himself the pain of those who are unintentionally but inevitably harmed by his resolute good deed. It is not enough to take his own chances and pay in himself the price of obedience. He must bear also the burden of those who willingly or not help pay for the good he does and whose sacrifice may be greater than his own. It is an awesome experience to obey God in those arenas where the ultimate human issues are contested. But it is infinitely more terrible to be challenged by God in those arenas and disobey him.

6

Justice and Community

We have now stressed sufficiently the primacy of distributive justice in the concrete human situation and have explored some of the implications of this premise. As we move from this emphasis to a quest for the Christian goal beyond justice, we should do so not by an abrupt turn but by cautious modulation, lest we leave the impression that distributive justice and Christian love are completely detached and wholly dissimilar modes of human relations. We have considered the primacy of an Aristotelian—a giving-to-each-man-his-due—justice as prerequisite to all human obligations. We have seen that in the racial field this justice relates to such matters as housing, voting, the use of public accommodations, employment, job promotion on merit, desegregated schools, etc. We have concluded that if the white Christian defaults the demands of this elementary justice in his dealings with the Negro —either by denying the Negro justice or by refusing to help him secure it—his protestations and pretenses of Christian love desecrate both love and justice. It is hypocritical and futile for a Christian to aspire to the love made known in Christ when he still falls short of the human obligations defined by Aristotle. Therefore we have said that in the concrete human situation Christian love can never be less than justice.

If, however, we halt here and refuse to be concerned about human relations beyond distributive justice we give to justice not only the primacy due to it but also the finality it does not deserve. Justice should be honored and served, not worshiped; it is penultimate, not ultimate. To treat justice as though it were ultimate as well as primary is to transform a good thing into an idol. This is the satanic temptation which abides in racial justice and there are civil rightists who succumb to it. For these civil rightists all things are weighed in the scales of justice and nothing is too sacred to be sacrificed to justice. But for Christians there must be a goal beyond equalizing justice. The prophet Micah, to whom we referred earlier, put justice first in his memorable summary of the highest religious insights of his time: "He has showed you, O man, what is good; and what does the LORD require of you but to do justice, and to love kindness, and to walk humbly with your God."[1] But apparently Micah arranged his trio of moral values in their ascending order and in that order justice was first but not highest. The Apostle Paul went further in his hierarchy of values: ". . . but the greatest of these is love."[2] And for Christians Jesus Christ expressed the ultimate effect of love: "that they may all be one; even as thou, Father, art in me, and I in thee, that they also may be in us, so that the world may believe that thou hast sent me."[3] The goal of the Christian in the racial struggle is not equality but a community to which equality is integral, not justice but a love which subsumes justice.

I am indebted to Philip C. Jessup, a judge of the international court of justice, for a quotation from Majid Khadduri, the educator and author: "Law is a system of social control established for the purpose of maintaining an ordered society among men." Jessup said of this statement: "Mark that it is not a system merely for maintaining order, but for maintaining an 'ordered society.' "[4] A modification of Khadduri's statement serves our purpose. The Christian goal in the racial struggle is not justice but a just society, with stress on the word "society." The end of Christian action is not merely an equitable distribution of goods, services, and opportunities but a society in which individuals find, form, enjoy, and mutually profit from their association with each other. In the popular word the aim is integration—a just *society*. Or, to use a word more meaningful to Christians than "society," what the Christian seeks in and beyond the racial struggle is a just community, with

---

1. Micah 6:8.
2. 1 Corinthians 13:13b.
3. John 17:21.
4. Philip C. Jessup, "Sticking the World Together," *Saturday Review* (February 1, 1964), p. 17.

stress on the word "community." Therefore we can now add a fifth
proposition to the four laid down in the previous chapter, a proposition which modifies everything said thus far in these pages: 5. *In
the concrete human situation the ultimate Christian goal is neither
justice nor mercy but a community which includes and goes beyond both.*

We noted earlier that the Negro's campaign for his civil rights
has inevitably estranged Negroes and whites from each other. This
occurs because such fraternity as has existed between the races in
the past was usually a frail, unhealthy paternalism based on assumptions of inferior and superior races. Interracial community in
the United States cannot come until sentimental, deceptive paternalism goes and paternalism will go only as justice comes. Therefore though the chasms which separate the races change their form
and appear more threatening as justice is pursued they are actually
no deeper and—for the Negro, at least—no more dangerous than
those which separated the races under a paternalistic system. The
Christian should not want to preserve or seek to restore a system
which calls up nostalgic white memories but which kept the Negro
debased. For the Christian there should be nothing threatening or
deplorable in the collapse of a human relationship which has been
harmful to the Negro, to the white man, and to the possibility of
their developing a mutually beneficial society. The paternalism
which precludes fraternity must go.

What should disturb Christians is the possibility that the collapse of paternalism as a social pattern will be followed, not by
community but by a deep, destructive, and permanent alienation of
the races, by a kind of spiritual apartheid in which the races each
enjoy justice but in which they do not share a common community.
An unfortunate mood develops among some white and Negro
champions of the Negro's civil rights campaign. In effect in their
preoccupation with distributive justice they are returning to a new
version of the Plessy *v.* Ferguson "separate but equal" doctrine of
race relations. In its 1954 desegregation of public schools the
United States Supreme Court repudiated the philosophy of that
doctrine. But the principle now returns in a new guise—a willingness on the part of some civil rightists to settle for an equality
which falls short of community. "Having" has priority over "be-

longing" but Negroes must not renounce, even if they must post-pone, the benefits of belonging in order to have. And though the white humanitarian secularist may be willing to limit his quest to a desegregation which fulfills the demands of equalizing justice, the white Christian must seek beyond justice an integrated community.

This means that the range of Christian action which seeks more than justice is more restricted than that of the action which seeks only justice. The stream of Christian action has justice as one of its confining, empowering, and directing banks and love as the other. On the one side the primary yet not imperial demands of distributive justice; on the other that love which always seeks the healing of those wounds which tragically divide men. On the one side the agencies of equality; on the other the powers and blessings of community. Outside these bounds Christian action ceases to be Christian. We have examined the demands of one of the banks—distributive justice; we must now examine the restrictions and possibilities of the other bank—uniting love.

We must note in passing a dangerous and disturbing development in the civil rights movement—a contempt for any testing of methods which seems to interfere with the obtaining of results. In an address before the Chicago chapter of the National Association of Housing and Redevelopment Officials on January 29, 1962, Mr. Saul Alinsky, executive director of the Industrial Areas Foundation, said, "Any so-called organization which spends a great deal of its time discussing means and ends, always winds up on its end without any means." We could permit Mr. Alinsky such a fillip as a passing jest were it not for persistent and convincing evidence that this view is one of the foundations on which he bases his whole philosophy of urban organization. By this principle whatever method is required, whatever means produces the desired end, automatically becomes legitimate. Mr. Alinsky's flippant remark about means and ends could be ignored but it has become too popular to be ignored. He has convinced a large number of Christians interested in urban organization that there is only one question to put to a given method: "Does it work?"

There are no chapters in the Christian church's history more tragic or more shameful than those in which it concluded that good ends justify any means. The church, Roman Catholic and Protestant, became not only inhumane but also blasphemous in those periods when it concluded that the good ends it sought could properly be secured by ends which in themselves could be considered evil but which were redeemed by the good purposes they served. So the church "for good cause" deprived men of their dignity, their freedom, their life. It is a hard-earned but evidently quickly forgotten lesson of church history that men play God and procure evil when they sanctify all methods which seem to promote their good purposes or which in fact achieve those purposes. Man in his finiteness is a creature who cannot be trusted to decide when and to what extent he shall sacrifice the integrity, the human rights, even the life itself of members of his kind for purposes he concludes are good. The Christian's right to deal as he pleases with his fellowman for purposes he knows to be good should be restricted by his awareness of his own finiteness and by his knowledge that every life—however wicked, however useless—is as sacred and inviolable as his own.

For our present purpose theoretical debates about means and ends are resolved by the finiteness and partiality of distributive justice. It is not ultimate and therefore does not permit man the use of whatever means he chooses—or even all means that work in his search for justice. Distributive justice is a legitimate goal but is not an end in an ultimate sense. Treat it as though it were, sacrifice everything to it, and it becomes a demon. The quest for distributive justice must always be regulated by the quest for a just community. Whatever is not just must by the primacy of justice be automatically omitted from the Christian's quest for community. Whatever destroys or prevents community must be on principle eliminated from the struggle for justice.

If community is the ultimate goal of Christian action, violence in all of its forms must be excluded from acceptable methods of Christian action in the struggle for racial justice. Simply defined violence means the exertion of harmful physical force against a human being. In this generation the Negro's fight for freedom and equality has been non-violent. Negro and white civil rightists have not only refused to initiate violent acts but have thus far also refused to respond to violence with violence. There have been two reasons for this repudiation of violence. In the main Negro and white Christians have rejected violence as an instrument of justice because they believe or sense that violence precludes community and that only through non-violence can oppression be overthrown and the opportunity for reconciliation be preserved. In his "How My Mind Has Changed" article in *The Christian Century* in 1960 Martin Luther King, Jr., stressed the power of non-violent resistance to overthrow oppression and its power to unite the oppressor and his victim: "A few months ago I had the privilege of traveling to India. The trip had a great impact on me personally and left me even more convinced of the power of non-violence. It was a marvelous thing to see the amazing results of a non-violent struggle. India won her independence, but without violence on the part of Indians. The aftermath of hatred and bitterness that usually follows a violent campaign is found nowhere in India. Today a mutual friendship based on complete equality exists between the Indian and British people within the commonwealth."[5] Similarly King and those who share his philosophy have one eye on justice and the other on community. It could be said that this part of the civil rights movement—that part sincerely committed to non-violent resistance—is nearsighted in the eye it fastens on justice and farsighted in the eye it turns toward community; but the important fact is that both eyes are used and both objectives sought.

For some civil rightists, however, the rejection of violence as a weapon in the battle for racial justice is a temporary strategy, not a fundamental and unalterable moral commitment. They know that the Negro is outnumbered ten to one and that few whites, however much they sympathize with the Negro, will join him in physical rebellion against his white oppressors. They know that the white man possesses the weapons which would be needed in a bloody revolution. They know that every effort by the Negro to overthrow his oppressor by physical force has ended disastrously. They know that nothing would please brutal white bigots more than an opportunity to unleash their full fury against the Negro. They know that a turn toward violence could sharply reverse the Negro's progress toward freedom and equality. Therefore these civil rightists preach and practice non-violence—not because it is the only morally de-

5. Martin Luther King, Jr., "How My Mind Has Changed," *The Christian Century* (April 13, 1960), pp. 440–441.

fensible method of protest, not because it preserves an opportunity for reconciliation—because it works in the struggle for justice and because at this juncture in history nothing else will work. Such civil rightists are not dedicated to non-violence but to whatever tool serves their purposes. Today that tool is non-violence; conceivably, for them, tomorrow's tool may be violence.

There are civil rightists who think they are in one of these camps but are actually in the other. They serve in movements which are in principle practitioners of non-violent resistance but they in fact practice non-violence as a temporary expediency. Not long ago I heard a high-level officer of a non-violent organization say in a public meeting: "Of course we are non-violent. I say to my people: 'It's stupid to throw beer bottles at people who have machine guns.'" This is prudence, not non-violence. Prudence is a virtue but it should not represent itself falsely. It may seem a quibble over words to draw this distinction between contrasting commitments to non-violence—between those who practice it on moral grounds because it preserves the opportunity for community across racial lines and those who practice it as a temporary utility in the quest for justice. Why be concerned about the motivation which underlies non-violent racial protest so long as it remains the acceptable mood and method of protest?

The answer to this question is multiple. Such duplicity turns non-violent resistance from a conscientious Gandhi who sincerely believes in the sacredness of all life into a sniveling Uriah Heep who feigns one mood in order to practice another. Such dishonesty, if it becomes rampant, will degrade and discredit non-violent direct action. Give the white man ground for belief that the Negro bides his time, waiting until *he* has the weapons, and non-violent protest against racial oppression comes to its end as an effective instrument. Deception will destroy both the moral quality and the utilitarian value of non-violent direct action. A civil rights worker who pretends that he is non-violent when in fact he is merely crafty betrays the trust of those who faithfully work with him and destroys his communication with those white people who must work out with him the structures of a decent and equitable society. If non-violence becomes merely a camouflage for latent violence, such deception, when it is exposed, leads the whites whose oppressiveness may be softening to conclude that the Negro's struggle for justice and equality is in fact a battle for dominance and superiority. However irrational such a conclusion may seem, it should not be encouraged. Therefore Negro and white Christians engaged in the civil rights struggle should scrupulously repudiate violence. And they should do so not because violence will not work in the current scene but because it destroys that community which is the ultimate goal of Christians.

We have assumed on solid theoretical and practical evidence that American Negroes—whether Christian or not, whether committed to non-violence or not—will not in this generation be tempted by the slim possibility of overthrowing by physical force the racial oppressions they suffer in a white-dominated society. There will, of course, be sporadic instances of rebellion in which individuals or groups, harassed beyond endurance, strike back at their tormentors and oppressors. We can also expect that increasingly—as provocation continues—Negroes will defend themselves physically against physical assaults by whites. Nevertheless they are not strongly tempted to turn a non-violent revolution into a bloody one. If this is true of Negroes, it is no less true of those whites who are now throwing their weight on the Negroes' side in the search for racial justice. These whites do not in significant numbers consider violence a legitimate or expedient instrument of social change.

But those of us—Negro and white—who are committed to the battle for a racially just society are subject to several temptations which are much more subtle than violence and which are equally destructive of community. We must examine these lures which appear to serve justice but which fail the test of interracial community and of justice. For these temptations divert the Christian from his ultimate goal—a just society—by promising the Negro freedom and equality at the expense of community. Let us look swiftly, then, at some of those attitudes which just men as well as unjust use in attacking their opposition—attitudes which divert the attack on injustice from the evil men do to men themselves.

We must note first that the danger of devotion to a good cause is the possibility of developing in ourselves a bigoted fanaticism which condemns and dismisses men who are not similarly devoted. This is a warning which those of us who are fully committed to a crusade for racial justice need to hold constantly before our eyes. The danger is that, fixing a single eye on justice, we shall use justice as the criterion by which we arbitrarily divide men into hard categories of good and evil. By this doctrinaire test we then define a good man as one who—whatever else he may be—wholly accepts our understanding of the racial problem and surrenders himself unreservedly to our solution of the problem. All other men we put without distinction into another category. In this second group we lump rabid segregationists, conservatives, moderates, liberals—anyone who does not see the problem exactly as we see it and anyone who prefers remedies different from our own. The deeper our devotion to racial justice the greater is our need to guard ourselves against the temptation to classify men as good and evil, right and wrong, with no common, mutually inhabited gray area between them. Otherwise we find ourselves unfairly and unwisely repudiating those who say, "I accept your diagnosis of the racial problem but I do not accept your prescription for its solution." Or we foolishly, wastefully alienate those who say, "I'll demonstrate, sit-in, picket, boycott, for racial justice; but I refuse to indulge in general harassments which do not focus on particular issues." Men who seek justice are no more immune from fanaticism than are those who are the doers of injustice.

Let us point up this thought with one dramatic illustration. According to the *Clarion Herald,* newsweekly of the Archdiocese of New Orleans, comedian Dick Gregory stumbled into the trap of that kind of fanaticism in a May 1, 1965, speech which he made at a Bogalusa, Louisiana, civil rights rally. According to the *Clarion Herald,* as reported by Religious News Service on May 7, 1965, the comedian called Federal Bureau of Investigation Director J. Edgar Hoover "one of the lousiest dogs that ever lived" and condemned elderly Negroes of Bogalusa as "too lazy or scared to do anything about the civil rights movement." The report stated that Mr. Gregory went on to say that the civil rights movement cannot progress until they die, adding, "Lord knows, I hope it's soon." Emile Comar, associate editor of the Roman Catholic paper, wrote in his weekly column: "To rip into such men as Hoover with the switchbade verbal attacks is something less than judicious and opens wounds that well-grounded Negro leaders cannot easily mend. To denounce the elderly men and women of his own race because they do not have the vitality to fight the undeniably rough civil rights battle is deplorable. To wish them death so that Gregory might march over their bodies to whatever he sees as freedomland is unbelievable." Gregory has the right to criticize the F.B.I. It has not always served justice impartially in the South. He has the right to rebuke Uncle Tomism when it appears among Negroes. But in this speech the comedian let his frankness degenerate into acrimony and his judgments become ruthlessly fanatical.

Fanatical, either-or classifications of men are easily detected, identified, and denounced when they come from the radical right wing of our political and social orders. In the speech which launched his John Birch Society, the retired candymaker, Robert Welch, said about the structure and policy of his new extremist organization: "We are not going to have factions developing on the two-sides-to-every-question theme." Radical right organizations have two groups into which they put all men: communists and anti-communists; for them there are no intermediate categories. But we do not so readily detect this same will to classify when it appears in us. Those of us who seek a just society should not be naïvely confident that the righteousness of our cause will prevent our stumbling into an equally arbitrary and unjust categorizing of men. As the civil rights movement becomes more and more revolutionary, it will more and more demand the revolutionary mind— the mind which sees all men as friends or foes, "in" or "out," good or evil.

We need to resist this temptation consciously because there is something in our nature which encourages—perhaps even demands—the division of men into "we" and "they." In her remarkable book, *The Second Sex,* Simone de Beauvoir wrote: "Otherness is a fundamental category of human thought. Thus it is that no group ever sets itself up as the One without at once setting up the Other over against itself."[6] This need for a human duality, for "we" and "they" categories, may be a part of our nature, but it is nevertheless an evil for which the Christian faith is the specifi-

---

6. Simone de Beauvoir, *The Second Sex* (New York: Bantam Books, 1964), p. xvii.

cally indicated cure. The Christian religion honors individuality but at the same time insists that there is a human Oneness which transcends all Otherness and that there is a human finiteness which prohibits ultimate human judgments of men. Matthew 13:24-30—the parable of the wheat and the tares—has from the beginning of Christian history argued for toleration and rebuked those men who believe that they have God's power to distinguish human wheat from human tares and God's right to repudiate, even destroy, those men identified as tares. We must not permit devotion to racial justice—a good thing—to degenerate into that blasphemous fanaticism which divides men into categories of good and evil. Justice in its inclusive sense does not lie in that direction and, obviously, such fanaticism precludes community.

Arbitrary divisions of men into hard and fast categories of good and evil on the basis of single, simple tests encourages a second betrayal of justice and community. In the racial struggle we are tempted to subvert justice and community by projecting the whole blame for racial injustice on those we have labeled evil. The word "scapegoating" and the mood and behavior which it identifies come to us from Leviticus 16:20-22: "And when he has made an end of atoning for the holy place and the tent of meeting and the altar, he shall present the live goat; and Aaron shall lay both his hands upon the head of the live goat, and confess over him all the iniquities of the people of Israel, and all their transgressions, all their sins; and he shall put them upon the head of the goat, and send him away into the wilderness by the hand of a man who is in readiness. The goat shall bear all their iniquities upon him to a solitary land; and he shall let the goat go in the wilderness." Psychologically scapegoating means the projection of one's own sense of guilt or frustration on some thing other than oneself, usually some available and vulnerable human being. The person who has an unbearable and unmanageable sense of personal guilt or who is baffled by life finds a likely candidate on whom he can unload his guilt and his bewilderment. Then, having transferred the blame for his own intolerable feelings of sinfulness and incompetence to the victim, he must destroy the victim, drive it psychologically if not physically "into the wilderness."

In its broader sociological sense scapegoating means the indicting of a race, a class, or a religion in order to relieve some other group of an unbearable sense of failure, incompetence, or frustration. Adolf Hitler, representative of the belief that Germans were not themselves responsible for their defeat in World War I, blamed the Jews for the nation's military catastrophes. The German people accepted the defenseless scapegoat Hitler offered them and eventually Jews within and outside of Germany were blamed for all German ills. When the Nazis slaughtered six million Jews before and during World War II, they took the demonic scapegoating process to its logical and psychological conclusion. They laid all of their guilt and their failures on the Jewish scapegoat and then sought to destroy it, to drive it "into the wilderness."

Civilized men, when they give sober thought to this matter, repudiate scapegoating as such and in its entirety, whatever or whoever the victim may be. They know that the transference of guilt and frustration to an innocent or even to an evil victim is unjust. They know moreover that the projection of guilt and frustration actually does more harm than good to the person who thus tries to shift blame from himself to someone else. His remorse, bitterness, and anxiety are not absolved by projection; instead they are submerged and their subtle effects on the person become more, not less pernicious.

The Christian man, if he is faithful to his gospel, must go a long step beyond the merely civilized man in repudiating in principle all scapegoating. For he will remember that only one man, Jesus Christ, was innocent enough to take upon himself voluntarily the sins of the world. This was his own free act in obedience to the revealed will of his Father. No one else has been worthy or able to assume the iniquities, the transgressions, and the sins of the world. No one else has been ordained by God to do it. Jesus Christ became the Lamb of God, gladly submitting to the will of God, not a scapegoat compelled by men to bear their sins. God and only God can lay the burdens of men upon one man. He did so only once and then only when the victim assented. To scapegoat, to lay the blame for our sin and frustration upon someone else, is to play God; and man is never more sinful, never more traitorous to himself and his fellowman, than when he plays God. To scapegoat is to seek a substitute Christ, as though the Lamb of God were not enough to take away the sins of the world.

Moreover, Christian belief in the inviolability of the individual —his sacredness, if you will—should compel the Christian to repudiate in principle and to avoid in practice all scapegoating. It does not matter how wicked the available victim, how perfectly he may symbolize a specific evil, how deserving he may seem to be destroyed, to be driven "into the wilderness," he is still God's child and the fallen brother of "good" men. There is something in the ugliest and cruelest of men which deserves respect if we respect ourselves, the faded but indelible stamp of his Creator if nothing else. However vile he may be personally, however brutal his treatment of other men, to treat him as a thing is to rebuke the God who made this fallen creature in his own image. Dostoevsky in his *Crime and Punishment* should have taught us—if the Bible did not—that no matter how worthless a life may seem in man's sight, it should never be used against its will for any purpose, however worthy the purpose. When we conclude that the worthless, vile, or wicked life has no rights in itself and is therefore available to be used as we please—we ourselves release demons which will eventually destroy us.

What does this have to do with us? We do not scapegoat Jews or Negroes. We do not condemn the communists for everything that goes wrong in the world. We try not to blame our wives, husbands, or friends for our misfortunes. We slam a door now and then, kick a fence, scold the dog, curse the fates. But we laugh at ourselves afterward and no great harm is done. Is this all? I think not. Indeed I suspect that those of us who are most involved in trying to rescue Jews and Negroes from vicious scapegoating are ourselves greatly tempted to scapegoat the oppressors of Jews and Negroes. We gather up the long, convoluted history of racial oppression in this country, roll it into a neat little ball, personalize it, and call it Governor George C. Wallace. We blame Selma, Alabama's sheriff Jim Clark or Birmingham's "Bull" Connor for all white hatred and brutality. We make a whipping boy out of white Baptists living in the Black Belt. In Chicago we blame public school superintendent Benjamin Willis for the segregated schools which help blight the lives of Negro children in this great metropo-

lis. Are Wallace, Clark, and Connor evil men in their racial practices? Indeed, they are. Are white Baptists in the Black Belt the
soil out of which much of this evil grows? Indeed, they are. Are
Benjamin Willis' administrative blunders responsible for continuing segregation in Chicago's schools? Indeed, they are. We choose
such people and others like them for our scapegoats, the deposito-
ries for our guilt, our victims, our "things," because they are already somewhat guilty. Since they are guilty they become visible,
vulnerable, and available sacrifices for our own sins and frustra-
tions. But their guilt, however great it may be, does not absolve
ours when we forget that they too are God's children, that
they too bear in them deeply hidden the stamp of their Creator and Father, and exploit them for purposes we believe wholly
good, entirely pure. Christian love does not rejoice in the evil it
discovers in men, but guilt does. Guilt not only demands the company misery loves; it also tries to use that company as an absolu-
tion.

It must be noted that we dress up our scapegoating in genteel
terms. When we focus the racial problem on a personality we say
that we are merely developing a symbol on which to concentrate
our righteous protest against racial injustice. The protest—so we
justify ourselves—would fail if we did not have a visible symbol to
attack. This argument is false on two counts: it is immoral and it
is impractical. Immoral, because whatever term we use as we load
on someone else the whole racial guilt we are in fact using people
as means, as instruments, as things. Impractical, because if we
symbolize the racial oppression of our day in one man or a group
of men and destroy that man or that group, the problem itself
remains unchanged, perhaps untouched. By focusing on the few
whose sin is flagrant and whose guilt is obvious, we divert
attention—ours and that of others—from the general sin and the
common guilt.

The scapegoating of any man for any purpose under any name
is psychologically perilous, morally indefensible, and socially in-
effective. Unless we renounce it per se, its subtleties in the concrete
human situation will be too much for us. Evil men are by Christian
definition men for whom Christ died. To use them for any good
purpose as though they being evil had no rights in themselves, as

though they were the devil's mistake delivered into our hands for righteousness' sake, is to question the wisdom, love, and sacrifice of that Christ whom Christians profess as Lord and need as Savior. Scapegoating is not a permissible instrument in the struggle for racial justice; it fails the ultimate test, the test of community.

If in our devotion to justice we classify men as good and evil and project the whole blame for racial injustice on those we have condemned as evil, we are then prepared to treat with contempt those who oppose us or who do not surrender to our view and our method. In the July 20, 1964, issue of *Christianity and Crisis,* a biweekly Christian journal of opinion, Stephen C. Rose, editor of *Renewal,* wrote: "Unquestionably there are well intentioned persons—ministers, social workers and citizens of Woodlawn—who have been deeply hurt by the raucous and rude attitude of those who advance T.W.O. (The Woodlawn Organization, a Chicago community group) as the ultimate savior of the community." In this statement Mr. Rose avoided value judgments; he did not say whether or not he approves and advocates the use of rudeness as an instrument of social change. But whatever Mr. Rose's position, there are ministers, social workers, and political scientists who believe that rough, insolent acts are indispensable and therefore legitimate weapons in an attack on intransigent social structures. As the contest for control of innercity organization intensifies and the racial struggle accelerates in the United States the cult of the rude is liable to increase.

The incivility about which we are concerned here involves something more than a lack of genteel manners or an absence of the common courtesies. It goes beyond that wholesome frankness which is required in the solution of personal and social conflicts. We are thinking rather of the use of incivility as a calculated, deliberate method in human relations. We are thinking of premeditated contumacy employed as a tactical device. At the Institute on Social Change in a Democratic Society held at Norman, Oklahoma, May 2-5, 1965, Dr. August Meier, professor of history at Roosevelt University, Chicago, Illinois, described the three assumptions which according to sociologists underlie all approaches to social change: (1) The Consensus Theory—an appeal to the people's conscience, to their native goodwill, their ideals, their political and religious creeds. (2) The Conflict Theory—the use of power to overthrow power in seeking social change. (3) The Competing Interests Theory—a search for the middle ground, for the compromise which will preserve the interests of competing groups. Obviously it is possible to combine aspects of all three of these approaches in a single effort to change an unjust social structure. Obviously also none of these approaches can on principle be rejected as unchristian. All three approaches can be used creatively or destructively. But Dr. Meier went on to say that the conflict theory of social change—which he prefers—requires incivility in human relations if it is to succeed. He contended that coarse acts disrespectful of people, traditions, and institutions break down barriers in human relations and achieve positive results which can be achieved in no other way. Is this true? Is rudeness an optional instrument for Christians in the civil rights struggle or in any other effort to change unjust social patterns?

If rudeness meant nothing more than a lack of the social graces, a default in etiquette, a disregard for the social conventions, a temperamental outburst, we could give this matter a quick dismissal. But the contempt for persons and things which this cult recommends as a legitimate form of direct action has grave moral, personal, and social consequences. The adjective "rude" does not in any of its synonyms commend itself favorably to the Christian conscience or to the good sense of sociologists who seek a just society. To be rude is to be uncivilized, uncivil, barbarous, discourteous, coarse, vulgar, impudent, insolent, disrespectful. Each of these synonyms expresses an attitude and defines a conduct denounced by Christian ethics and rejected by those social theories which seek a just society rather than mere equality as the ultimate goal in human relations.

Therefore on two grounds we must disqualify the use of calculated rudeness in securing social change. First, it assaults that part of its victim which should be beyond assault—the irreducible sacredness and integrity of the individual. The contemptuous act dismisses the person as a person. This, in fact, is one of the specific meanings of rudeness: it seeks by contempt to destroy the essential being of the person it attacks. Not content with removing the foe as foe, rudeness attempts beyond this to destroy the personhood of the foe. The deliberate insult reveals in the offender the willingness to turn the "Thou" which always exists in every human being into a contemptible "It" which can be treated as one wills. Thus the insolent act may carry the flag of some good cause—it often does—but it betrays that cause. For what cruel and contemptuous conduct really serves is not the good cause but the pride and the power-hunger of the one who uses it to degrade his fellowman and thus exalt himself. Scratch the surface of the man who treats his adversaries contemptuously and you will discover that he is not so much interested in securing justice for Negroes and poor whites as he is in having his own way whatever the consequences. In the name of a good cause he will do a great evil to satisfy his own hunger for power.

Second, direct action which treats the adversary contemptuously destroys indispensable lines of communication and prevents or indefinitely postpones those consultations which can restore the community which is necessarily disrupted by controversy. In the civil rights movement and in attempts to bring about other social changes the agitator plays an important role; but so, also, does the negotiator. If the agitator overplays his role, if he treats his opponent contemptibly, he makes it difficult, sometimes impossible, for men on both sides of the social conflict to sit about the table and put the pieces of a disrupted social structure back together in more just patterns.

Christians engaged in the struggle for racial justice should not conceal explosive conflicts of opinions and interests under heavy blankets of artificial gentility. Nor—as can be done—should they use suavity to stifle healthful controversy. On the contrary the dimension and the cruciality of today's racial problems are such that firmness and frankness are warranted, indeed required, as men grapple with those problems. But we should not confuse frankness and rudeness; they are not identical. We should not confuse firmness and callousness; they are not the same. Rudeness is not merely a tactical blunder which cuts off communication, widens the gulfs between men, and prevents the development of community. It also offends that God who created man in his own image and gave to each man an inviolable self. When the Apostle told the

Corinthians that "love is not arrogant or rude," he was not thinking of the niceties of good manners. He was saying at a much
deeper level that Christian love always seeks to preserve the essential self of the other person—even though that person be a foe—
and that Christian love seeks the unity of all men and not the
peace which comes from the spiritual annihilation of some men.
For the Christian rudeness is out as an instrument of ethical
action.

Nearly 60 years ago Kelly Miller, Howard University dean and
sociologist, asked, "What power is there in Christianity to wean
men from race prejudice?"[7] This was not—as it might be if raised
by a Negro now—a cynical question. Miller was in earnest; he
believed that somewhere in Christianity there is a moral equivalent
of race prejudice. Christians who see in racism "the full inward-
ness of the situation" that William James saw in militarism know
that Kelly Miller's question is always basic, always relevant. They
know that it gets to the deepest roots of the racial problem and
that we must always be seeking for the answer to that question.
But Christians who are alert to what is happening in the world of
racial conflict know also that Miller's fundamental question has
been pushed into the background by equally relevant and more
practical questions. The Negro today is not so much concerned
with how to stop the white man from hating him as he is with how
to keep the white man from strangling him in the ghetto, killing
him in his home and church, locking him out of the nation's house.
Prejudice can wait; what has to be destroyed now is the political
and social oppression which has race prejudice as one of its causes
and one of its excuses. And there is no longer any question about
it; prejudice can be by-passed, out-flanked, by men who sincerely,
relentlessly, seek a just society for all men.

The exigencies of our time give the practical questions priority
over the philosophical and psychological ones. These same exigencies compel concerned Christians to reorder the questions to which
they give priority. The what-can-I-do question takes priority over
the what-can-I-believe question. To bury oneself in speculations

7. Kelly Miller, *Race Adjustment* (New York: The Neele Publishing Company,
1910), p. 148.

about the nature and cure of race prejudice or in theoretical discussions of the Negro's right to a full, unrestricted place in the nation's body or in endless debates of insoluble theological issues—to do this while the racial storm erupts all about us—can be in these times a craven flight from reality and a callous betrayal of the Negro's rights and hopes. The primary question is not—as with Miller—what Christianity can do about race prejudice but what white Christians should do to help end the degrading of Negroes. And—to return to the principal theme of this work—the question is how white Christians can escape from that quandary in which for more than three centuries they have floundered in an ambivalent, vacillating relation to Negroes.

The relevant and immediate question, then, drives us not to words but to the world, not to preachments but to practices, not to the reading of books about Christian action but to deeds which liberate the white Christian and help rescue the Negro from those chains still forged and fitted on the Negro by a white society. If not for the Negro's sake, then for his own sake the white Christian must invest his life in activities which promote a racially just society. Many Christians have not accepted the Christian view of the racial problem because they have not lived as Christians in the midst of that problem. The interplay between opinion and habit, belief and deed, is often exactly opposite from what we commonly suppose. We put the ideological cart before the behavioral horse. We assume that thoughts, opinions, speculations, always come first and that deeds and habits follow afterward. The reverse is often true. It is far more accurate, a far better reading of our nature, to say that our moods, the set of our minds, our customary intellectual reactions, are the products of our deeds. We think as we do because we act as we do. The deed is mother of the thought; action tests speculation. We find ourselves not through a Cartesian exploration of our interior being but through Kierkegaardian acts. As Christians we become in doing. The active racist may be an evil man but he is a man; the silent, passive Christian may harmlessly wear the name of Christian but he is neither a man nor a Christian. The Christian life is a function, not a formality.

This is not to say, of course, that the Christian life is sheer activism in the racial field or in any other social context. The

Christian life has personal as well as social dimensions and the individual has with himself, with nature, and with God relationships which are properly termed religious. But as a social being man's religious life is actualized by what he does in the world of men. We have concluded that in the racial field the Christian must not only act and take the consequences of action but must keep his actions within the restrictive banks of the primacy of justice on the one side and the ultimacy of community on the other. He cannot as a Christian do less than what is just; he must not as a Christian by evil deeds or good ones destroy or prevent community. On one side of him are history's abundant reminders that appeals to conscience and creed, that reliance upon persuasion and voluntaryism, seldom get justice done. He will therefore employ in his devotion to racial justice those instruments which civilized men provide for the redress of wrongs: legislation, litigation, and election. Where these fail he will use those forms of social protest which are extralegal: demonstrations, boycotts, petitions, and the various "ins" which challenge the exclusion of the Negro. And where local law has itself become the instrument of racial oppression and exploitation the Christian—white or Negro—will under the compulsion of conscience break the law which is no law. He will not do so recklessly or with contempt for society, but he will not permit what God wills for the Negro and what the United States Constitution guarantees to him to be withheld by discriminatory customs which have arbitrarily assumed the aegis of law. The civil disobedience in which Christians can engage and remain Christian is not anarchism, not a flippant or contemptuous defiance of society's legal structure. In its Christian usage civil disobedience is not so much the breaking of law as it is a selective obedience of law. Inferior, humiliating, unjust laws are repudiated by obedience to superior civil or moral laws. Open to us in the search for justice are legal, extralegal, and superlegal instruments, each of which should be used as occasions require. For Christians cannot move toward community—their ultimate goal—over a terrain occupied by injustice. Unless they do justly they must forfeit all hope for community.

But the actions of a Christian in the world of racial conflict are disciplined and focused by his paramount concern for a community which includes Negroes and whites as equals. What the Christian does and what he refuses to do in the civil rights movement are governed by two self-evident facts. First, however necessary force of one kind or another may be in implementing racial justice, some forms of coercion—physical and psychical—kill all prospects for community. Whatever other men may do, the Christian, obedient to his Lord's desire that the people be one, will exclude from his struggle for justice all acts deepening the wounds which alienate men from men. He will not be deceived by those sentimental semblances of community which degrade Negroes and whites, nor will he regret their disappearance. He will not forget the primacy of justice, but neither will he betray the ultimacy of community. The Christian will not overlook the possibility that there may be tough wisdom in the Apostle Paul's declaration that we must not be overcome by evil but must overcome evil with good. The use of evil to overcome racial evil is no solution but is merely the exchange of one problem for another.

Second, it is a self-evident fact that no amount of coercion can produce community. To speak of forcing men into community is to use mutually contradictory terms. We therefore do not look to the law or to any extralegal social pressures to create for us that relation between men which is beyond equalitarianism and mutual respect. Here we must rely on another kind of power—internal rather than external, spiritual rather than material, love rather than law. In the thick of what becomes more and more a racial revolution love seems a harmless, beautiful, but impotent instrument. But Christian love is no tame sentiment, no mere emotional glow, no delicate combination of warmth and helplessness. In those life-situations where men abuse and exploit men Christian love appears in the rugged form of justice and where men are estranged by conflict and competing interests Christian love appears as reconciliation. And usually there are coincidental situations in which Christian love must at once satisfy the needs of both. The social revolutions of our day do not call for those methods which destroy the identity and the sacred rights of the person and which shatter human oneness. Rather the social revolutions cry out in our time for Christian love which eliminates the gross inequalities men heap upon each other and which binds up and heals the deep wounds which separate men from men. Nothing in the present racial upheaval changes the role of the Christian. That role is not to manipulate the conflicts inherent in the human situation but to remove those inequities which compound human conflict and to embody among men the message of reconciliation. However somber, perilous, and chaotic the times, this remains the mandate for white Christians.